Festive Food
For Vegetarians

FESTIVE FOOD
FOR VEGETARIANS

Linda Majzlik

GREEN
PRINT

First published in 1991 by
Green Print
an imprint of The Merlin Press
10 Malden Road, London NW5 3HR

ISBN 1 85425 073 6

Phototypeset by Computerset Ltd., Harmondsworth, Middlesex.

Printed in England by Biddles Ltd., Guildford, Surrey
on recycled paper.

CONTENTS

◊   ◊   ◊

INTRODUCTION

◊   ◊   ◊

Finding out that a vegetarian diet does not consist entirely of nut roast and lentils can come as a great shock to a lot of meat eaters. In fact, I am constantly asked the question 'But what DO you cook for "such-and-such" occasion?' This is particularly true of the festive season, when for some reason it seems unbelievable that you can have a celebration meal without the traditional turkey as a centrepiece.

Bearing this in mind, this book of celebration foods sets out to illustrate that a vegetarian diet is neither boring nor tasteless. It is in fact quite the reverse, being infinitely more exciting than the traditional meat-and-two-veg variety.

The theme of this book is the various celebrations throughout the year and how to celebrate them with healthy and delicious vegetarian foods. Besides being meat-free most of the recipes are low in fat and sugar and high in fibre. None of the recipes have added salt.

The book is divided into three sections. Part 1 deals with the Christmas festive season in general and contains recipes for starters, main courses, accompanying dishes and desserts for you to choose from to create your own special meals. Alternatively, follow one of the suggested menus which have been devised using dishes which compliment each other. Either way you will end up with a tasty and attractive alternative to the traditional spread. Lots of the more usual festive foods will also be found in this section – for example, Christmas puddings and mincemeat. The recipes for these however, contain no suet and have a much lower sugar content than the traditional alternatives.

Part 2 concentrates on set meals and ideas for other celebrations which occur throughout the year and also includes a section on celebration drinks to serve with your meals.

Finally, Part 3 provides recipes for making edible presents. There's something very special about receiving a beautifully packaged home-made gift of food which has been lovingly prepared. There are lots of occasions throughout the year when such a gift would make an appropriate present for a special friend or relative. St. Valentine's Day, Easter, birthdays, Mother's Day, Father's Day and Christmas are just a few.

With the slightly cranky image of the vegetarian diminishing and the trend towards healthier eating continuing, maybe more people will now begin to think about giving up eating meat, especially after sampling some wholesome vegetarian cuisine.

A NOTE ON INGREDIENTS

◊   ◊   ◊

The following applies to the ingredients used in the recipes in this book:

Cheeses – Most supermarkets and health food shops stock a whole range of
  vegetarian cheeses which are made with non-animal rennet.
Eggs – All eggs are free range size 3 unless otherwise stated.
Essences – Available from health food shops, essences are natural flavour-
  ings as opposed to 'extracts' which are synthetic.
Agar agar – A vegetable gelling and thickening powder which is a vege-
  tarian/vegan alternative to gelatine.
Herbs – Unless otherwise stated dried herbs are used in the recipes. If you
  prefer to use fresh herbs, remember to double the quantity given.
Milk – All milk is semi-skimmed.
Soy sauce – Choose a brand which is naturally fermented without the use of
  chemicals. Shoyu is a light soy sauce whilst tamari is dark and has a
  stronger flavour.
Worcester sauce – Buy from a health food shop as most supermarket brands
  contain anchovies.

N.B. Use either imperial or metric quantities; do not mix the two. All spoon
measures are level unless otherwise stated.

PART 1
FESTIVE FOOD FOR CHRISTMAS

CHRISTMAS AND THE FESTIVE SEASON

◊   ◊   ◊

This can be a daunting time of year even for the experienced cook – with so many things to remember, so many people to cater for and so little time for preparation. Planning ahead is the key to a relatively stress-free Christmas. Plan to shop for all the non-perishables as far in advance as is possible, leaving just the fresh foods to buy at the last moment.

Try to make good use of the freezer at this time, making up dishes when there is more time to spare and freezing until required. Certain festive foods need to be made well in advance in order for them to mature. For example the Christmas cake, Christmas pudding, mincemeat and cranberry sauce can all be made weeks in advance.

This section of the book deals entirely with festive foods and includes menus to help you plan your meals. Of course you might prefer to plan your own menus. Always try to balance meals carefully and aim for a good contrast of textures and flavours. For example avoid serving a main course made with pastry with a pastry-based dessert, or a fruit-based starter with a fruit dessert. It's also a good idea to have a light starter and dessert when serving a heavy main course.

Most of the recipes in this section serve either 4 or 6 people and can easily be adjusted to serve more. If you are catering for only 2 or 3 people the unused portions of the main courses can be individually wrapped and frozen.

Incidentally, apart from the Festive cracker, there is no reason why the main courses couldn't be made for other celebration dinners throughout the year. Frozen Brussels sprouts would have to be substituted for fresh ones in the Raised vegetable layered pie if making it out of season. Frozen peeled chestnuts can be used in all recipes requiring chestnuts. They may appear to be more expensive than fresh ones, but there is no wastage and they are convenient to use. Frozen chestnuts are available in supermarkets from approximately November until May. If they are unavailable, dried ones can be substituted. To use these soak them in water overnight, then rinse and place in a saucepan of water. Bring to the boil, cover and simmer for 10 minutes. Drain and then follow the recipe. You will need 6oz/175g dried chestnuts to make approximately 8oz/225g when reconstituted.

Finally, create a festive atmosphere for your guests by paying special attention to the table setting. Look out for suitable table cloths, table mats, serviettes and place name cards. Add a decorative centrepiece with candles for the finishing touch.

SOME SUGGESTED FESTIVE DINNER MENUS

◊   ◊   ◊

Menu 1
Hazelnut, cranberry and brandy paté with a salad garnish

Festive cracker
Roast potatoes
Brussels sprouts with chestnuts
Mixed vegetable platter
Cranberry and orange sauce

Christmas pudding with yoghurt

Menu 2
Pear and pistachio salad

Cranberry and orange nut loaf with orange and wine sauce
Roast potatoes
Carrot and ginger purée
Parsnip and apple purée
Mixed vegetable platter

Festive garland with yoghurt

Menu 3
Onion and sherry soup

Fruity chestnut strudel
Spiced parsnips with almonds
Jacket potatoes
Mixed vegetable platter
Bramley apple and clove sauce

Christmas pudding sundaes

Menu 4
Chilled melon soup

Chick pea, cranberry and Brazil nut pie
Roast potatoes
Roast parsnips

Fennel, carrot and courgette sauté
Mangetout
Apricot and ginger relish

Chestnut, sultana and brandy cheesecake

Menu 5
Chestnut soup

Mushroom, cranberry and walnut brioche
Mixed vegetables with almonds
Potato and spinach casserole
Roast parsnips

Iced Christmas bombe

Menu 6
Stilton, spinach and walnut spread with melba toast

Celebration paté loaf with mushroom and brandy sauce
Jacket potatoes
Brussels sprouts with chestnuts
Baked red cabbage with apples and sultanas

Melon with liqueur fruits

Menu 7
Orange, date and cashew nut cocktail

Pecan paté en croûte
Boiled potatoes with carrot and tahini sauce
Brussels sprouts gratin
French beans
Mangetout
Cranberry and orange sauce

Individual Christmas trifles

Menu 8
Pecan and wine paté with a salad garnish

Raised vegetable layered pie
Roast potatoes
Bread sauce
Mixed vegetable platter
Cranberry, apple and port sauce

Fig and orange pudding with orange and
  brandy sauce

Menu 9
Grapefruit, stilton and walnut cups

Lentil and nut roast with onion and
  paprika gravy
Potato and spinach purée
Celeriac and swede purée
Baked red cabbage with apples and
  sultanas
Cauliflower

Cranberry and orange tart with yoghurt

STARTERS

◊ ◊ ◊

CHILLED MELON SOUP (serves 4)

1 medium honeydew melon
5 fl.oz / 150ml fresh orange juice
2 fl.oz / 50ml white wine

1 rounded teaspoon demerara sugar
1 inch / 2¹/₂cm piece of stem ginger, finely
sliced

Cut the melon in half and using a melon baller make 12 melon balls and reserve. Remove the skin and pips from the melon. Chop the flesh and place in a liquidiser with the orange juice, wine and sugar. Blend until smooth. Refrigerate for a few hours until cold. Divide between 4 bowls and garnish each with melon balls and sliced ginger.

ONION AND SHERRY SOUP (serves 4)

1lb / 450g onions, peeled and chopped
17 fl.oz / 500ml water
3 fl.oz / 75ml medium sherry
1 tablespoon sunflower oil

1 teaspoon chervil
1 teaspoon soy sauce
¹/₂ teaspoon yeast extract
black pepper

Heat the oil and fry the onion for 10 minutes. Add the water, chervil, soy sauce and yeast extract and season with black pepper. Bring to the boil, then cover and simmer for 15 minutes. Remove from the heat and stir in the sherry. Allow to cool slightly, then liquidise until smooth. Return to the cleaned pan and reheat to serve.

CHESTNUT SOUP (serves 4)

8oz/225g shelled chestnuts, chopped
1 onion, chopped
1 dessertspoon sunflower oil
1 pint/600ml water
2 tablespoons sherry

1 teaspoon soy sauce
black pepper
$^1/_4$ teaspoon yeast extract
$^1/_4$ teaspoon ground mace

Heat the oil and gently fry the onion until softened. Add the chestnuts and fry for 1 minute. Add the remaining ingredients and stir well. Bring to the boil, then cover and simmer for 10 minutes. Remove from the heat and allow to cool slightly. Liquidise until smooth, then return to the cleaned pan and reheat to serve.

PECAN AND WINE PATÉ (serves 6)

4oz/100g pecans, grated
4oz/100g celery, finely chopped
2oz/50g millet
1 onion, finely chopped
1 garlic clove, crushed
1 egg, beaten
8 fl.oz/225ml water

2 fl.oz/50ml white wine
1 dessertspoon olive oil
1 teaspoon marjoram
1 teaspoon thyme
$^1/_4$ teaspoon yeast extract
black pepper

Heat the oil and gently fry the onion, garlic and celery until softened. Add the millet, water and yeast extract. Stir well and bring to the boil. Cover and simmer until the liquid has been absorbed. Remove from the heat, add the wine and liquidise until smooth. Stir in the pecans, egg, marjoram and thyme and season with black pepper. Mix thoroughly, then spread the mixture evenly in a lined and greased 7 inch/18cm round flan tin. Bake in a preheated oven at 180°C/350°F/Gas mark 4 for 60-70 minutes until golden and set. Cut into wedge shapes and serve hot or cold.

HAZELNUT, CRANBERRY AND
BRANDY PATÉ (serves 4)

3oz/75g hazelnuts, ground	1 egg, beaten
3oz/75g cranberry sauce	3 tablespoons brandy
2oz/50g fresh wholemeal breadcrumbs	1 tablespoon sunflower oil
2oz/50g long grain brown rice	1 teaspoon chervil
2oz/50g carrot, scraped and grated	1 teaspoon thyme
1 onion, finely chopped	1 teaspoon paprika
2 celery sticks, finely chopped	black pepper

Cook the rice until tender, then drain thoroughly. Heat the oil and gently fry the onion and celery until softened. Add the carrot and fry for 1 minute. Remove from the heat and add the cooked rice and the remaining ingredients. Mix thoroughly and put in a base lined and greased 7 inch/18cm loaf tin. Level the top and bake in a preheated oven at 170°C/325°F/Gas mark 3 for 40 minutes. Slide a sharp knife around the edges to loosen, then invert onto a baking tin and carefully remove the foil. Return to the oven and bake for a further 10 minutes until golden. Cut into slices and serve hot or cold.

STILTON, SPINACH AND
WALNUT SPREAD (serves 6)

3oz/75g blue stilton, mashed	3 spring onions, finely chopped
3oz/75g cottage cheese, mashed	1 tablespoon fresh parsley, chopped
2oz/50g frozen cooked chopped spinach, thawed	$\frac{1}{4}$ teaspoon grated nutmeg
1oz/25g walnuts, chopped	black pepper to taste

Mix all the ingredients together thoroughly. Divide between individual ramekin dishes. Spread onto crusty wholemeal French bread.

PEAR AND PISTACHIO SALAD (serves 4)

1 ripe avocado pear
1 just ripe dessert pear
$^1/_2$ bunch watercress
1oz/25g shelled pistachio nuts

1 dessertspoon lemon juice
1 teaspoon sunflower oil
black pepper
8 black grapes, quartered

Peel and stone the avocado and dice. Peel and core the dessert pear and dice. Place both pears in a mixing bowl. Mix the sunflower oil with the lemon juice and season with black pepper. Pour this over the pears. Reserve a few pistachios for garnish and add the rest to the pears. Toss together carefully. Trim the stalks from the watercress, divide the leaves between 4 sundae glasses and arrange the pear salad on the leaves. Garnish with the reserved pistachios and the quartered black grapes.

ORANGE, DATE AND CASHEW NUT COCKTAIL (serves 4)

4 oranges
8 fresh dates, finely sliced
4 tablespoons fresh orange juice

1oz/25g cashew nuts, roasted
ground cinnamon

Peel the oranges and break into segments. Remove all the membranes and pith and chop each segment into small chunks. Place in a bowl with the dates and orange juice. Refrigerate for a couple of hours, then divide between 4 sundae glasses. Sprinkle lightly with ground cinnamon and add the cashew nuts just before serving.

GRAPEFRUIT, STILTON AND WALNUT CUPS (serves 4)

2 grapefruit
4oz/100g blue stilton, cubed
4 lettuce leaves, shredded

2 cocktail gherkins, sliced
2oz/50g walnuts, halved

Cut the grapefruit in half and take out the segments. Remove the membrane from the segments and shells and discard. Chop the segments and mix with the stilton, gherkins and walnuts. Place some shredded lettuce in the bottom of each half shell and fill them with the mixture.

MAIN COURSES

◊ ◊ ◊

FESTIVE CRACKER (serves 6)

8oz/225g puff pastry

filling
4oz/100g carrot, scraped and grated
4oz/100g leek, finely shredded
2oz/50g Brazil nuts, grated
2oz/50g shelled chestnuts, grated
2oz/50g dried apricots, chopped
2oz/50g bulgar wheat
1oz/25g sunflower seeds
1oz/25g sultanas
1 egg, beaten

4 fl.oz/125ml boiling water
1 tablespoon sherry
1 dessertspoon soy sauce
1 dessertspoon vegetable oil
$^1/_2$ teaspoon yeast extract
$^1/_2$ teaspoon ground coriander
$^1/_2$ teaspoon paprika
$^1/_4$ teaspoon ground cinnamon
black pepper
milk
sesame seeds

Dissolve the yeast extract in the water, then add the bulgar wheat and allow to stand for 10 minutes. Heat the oil and gently fry the carrot and leek for a few minutes. Remove from the heat and add the soaked bulgar wheat together with the remaining filling ingredients. Roll out the pastry to a 14 × 12 inch/35 × 30cm oblong. Cut out small triangles from the edges of the 12 inch/30cm sides to give a serrated effect, and reserve these for decoration.

Place the filling along the centre of the pastry to within 2 inches/5cm of the serrated sides. Fold over the pastry to enclose the filling and place with the join underneath on a greased baking sheet. Pinch the sides together to form a cracker shape. Using a sharp knife make a diagonal pattern all over the top but do not cut through the pastry. Prick the pastry with a fork and brush with milk. Arrange the reserved pastry triangles on the top and sprinkle with sesame seeds. Bake in a preheated oven at 170°C/325°F/Gas mark 3 for 35-40 minutes until golden.

FRUITY CHESTNUT STRUDEL (serves 4)

12 10 × 8 inch/25 × 20cm sheets of filo
   pastry
4oz/100g shelled chestnuts, grated
4oz/100g mushrooms, wiped and
   chopped
4oz/100g cranberry sauce
2oz/50g dried apricots, sliced
2oz/50g carrot, scraped and grated
1 onion, finely chopped
2 sticks of celery, finely chopped

1 egg, beaten
1 tablespoon sunflower oil
1 teaspoon ground coriander
1 teaspoon paprika
1 teaspoon soy sauce
$^1/_4$ teaspoon ground mace
black pepper
extra sunflower oil
onion seeds and sesame seeds

Heat the tablespoonful of oil and gently fry the onion and celery until softened. Stir in the chestnuts and fry for a few seconds. Remove from the heat and add the mushrooms, apricots, carrot, egg, ground coriander, paprika, soy sauce and ground mace and season with black pepper. Mix thoroughly.

Put a sheet of filo pastry onto a sheet of cling film and brush lightly with sunflower oil. Place another sheet of filo on top, oil and repeat with a third sheet. Place half of the filling onto the pastry to within 1 inch/2$^1/_2$cm of the edges on the long sides. Arrange 3 more sheets of filo on top, lightly oiling between sheets. Spread the cranberry sauce along the centre. Cover with 3 lightly oiled sheets of filo and spread the remaining filling on the pastry to within 1 inch/2$^1/_2$cm of the long edges as before. Finish with the last 3 sheets of filo, lightly oiling between each sheet.

Fold the long edges of pastry towards the centre by pulling up the cling film. Place the strudel on a greased baking tray with the join underneath. Lightly oil the top and sprinkle with onion and sesame seeds. Cover with foil and bake in a preheated oven at 180°C/350°F/Gas mark 4 for 30 minutes. Remove the foil and bake for a further 10 minutes until golden and crispy.

CELEBRATION PATÉ LOAF (serves 6)

pastry
9oz/250g fine wholemeal self raising
  flour
3oz/75g sunflower margarine
1oz/25g Cheddar cheese, grated
¼ teaspoon cayenne pepper
milk
sesame seeds

filling
6oz/175g mixed nuts, grated
4oz/100g shelled chestnuts, grated
4oz/100g carrot, scraped and grated
4oz/100g mushrooms, wiped and finely
  chopped

1 onion, finely chopped
1 stick of celery, finely chopped
2 garlic cloves, crushed
2 eggs, beaten
1 tablespoon sunflower oil
1 dessertspoon soy sauce
1 rounded teaspoon chervil
1 rounded teaspoon thyme
1 teaspoon paprika
black pepper
6oz/175g cranberry sauce

Rub the margarine into the flour, then stir in the Cheddar and the cayenne pepper. Add enough milk to bind and turn out onto a floured board. Take three-quarters of the pastry and roll out to line a foiled and greased 9 inch/23cm loaf tin. Leave a large overhang of foil to enable the pie to be lifted out when cooked. Roll out the remaining piece of pastry to fit the top. Cut any leftover pastry into leaf shapes for decoration. Heat the oil and gently fry the onion, celery and garlic until softened. Remove from the heat and stir in the remaining ingredients, except the cranberry sauce. Mix thoroughly.

Spread half .the filling in the pastry case and press down firmly and evenly. Cover with the cranberry sauce and spread the remaining filling evenly on the top. Press down firmly. Place the pastry lid over the top and press the edges together with a fork. Prick the top all over with a fork, brush with milk and arrange the pastry leaves on top. Brush these with milk as well and sprinkle with sesame seeds. Cover with foil and bake in a preheated oven at 180°C/350°F/Gas mark 4 for 45 minutes. Uncover and bake for a further 15 minutes until golden on top. Remove from the oven and allow to cool in the tin for 5 minutes, then carefully lift out of the tin using the overhanging foil. Remove the foil and place the loaf on a serving dish. Serve hot cut into thick slices.

CRANBERRY AND ORANGE NUT LOAF WITH ORANGE AND WINE SAUCE (serves 6)

loaf
8oz/225g cranberry sauce
6oz/175g shelled chestnuts, grated
4oz/100g carrot, scraped and grated
2oz/50g walnuts, finely grated
2oz/50g almonds, finely grated
2oz/50g Brazil nuts, finely grated
2oz/50g hazelnuts, finely grated
2oz/50g fresh wholemeal breadcrumbs
1 onion, finely chopped
1 stick of celery, finely chopped
finely grated peel of 1 orange
2 eggs, beaten
1 tablespoon vegetable oil

1 dessertspoon Worcester sauce
1 teaspoon soy sauce
1 teaspoon chervil
1 teaspoon chives
black pepper
1 tablespoon flaked almonds

sauce
1/4 pint/150ml fresh orange juice
1/4 pint/150ml white wine
1 rounded dessertspoon arrowroot
1/2 teaspoon ground coriander
1/4 teaspoon ground mace
black pepper

Heat the oil and gently fry the onion, celery and orange peel until softened. Add the chestnuts and stir around for a minute or two. Remove from the heat and add the rest of the loaf ingredients except the flaked almonds. Grease and line the base of an 8 inch/20cm loaf tin. Sprinkle the flaked almonds evenly in the bottom. Spoon the loaf mixture into the tin, level the top and press down firmly. Cover with foil and bake in a preheated oven at 170°C/325°F/Gas mark 3 for 1½ hours. Remove the foil and bake for a further 15 minutes, until golden and firm in the centre.

Near the end of the cooking time make the sauce. Pour the orange juice and wine into a small saucepan, add the rest of the sauce ingredients and stir until smooth. Bring slowly to the boil, stirring all the time, and continue stirring until the sauce thickens. Keep warm.

Slice a sharp knife around the edges to loosen the loaf, then invert it onto a serving plate. Carefully remove the base lining. Cut the loaf into thick slices and pour the sauce over. Serve hot.

PECAN PATÉ EN CROÛTE (serves 4/5)

8oz/225g puff pastry	1 tablespoon sunflower oil
4oz/100g pecan nuts, grated	1 tablespoon sherry
2 sticks of celery, finely chopped	1 dessertspoon soy sauce
1 onion, finely chopped	1 teaspoon thyme
4oz/100g carrot, scraped and grated	1 teaspoon chervil
2oz/50g mushrooms, wiped and sliced	black pepper
1 garlic clove, crushed	milk
1 egg, beaten	sesame seeds

Heat the oil and gently fry the celery, onion and garlic until softened. Add the mushrooms and fry until the juices run. Remove from the heat and add the grated nuts, carrot, egg, sherry, soy sauce, thyme and chervil. Season with black pepper and mix thoroughly. Roll out the pastry to a 14 × 10 inch/35 × 25cm oblong.

Place the filling evenly along the centre. Fold the pastry over to enclose the filling and dampen the edges with milk to join. Place on a greased baking sheet with the join underneath. Brush with milk and make slits on the top in a criss-cross pattern. Use a sharp knife and be careful not to cut right through the pastry. Sprinkle with sesame seeds and bake in a preheated oven at 170°C/325°F/Gas mark 3 for 35-40 minutes until golden.

LENTIL AND NUT ROAST (serves 6)

loaf
4oz/100g brown lentils
1 small onion, finely chopped
4oz/100g celery, finely chopped
4oz/100g carrot, scraped and grated
2oz/50g walnuts, grated
2oz/50g Brazil nuts, grated
2oz/50g ground almonds
2 garlic cloves, crushed
2 eggs, beaten
1 tablespoon sherry
1 tablespoon sunflower oil

1 dessertspoon soy sauce
1 rounded teaspoon parsley
1 rounded teaspoon mixed herbs
1 teaspoon paprika
black pepper
1 tablespoon flaked almonds

filling
4oz/100g shelled chestnuts, grated
4oz/100g cranberry sauce
1 small onion, finely chopped
1 dessertspoon sunflower oil

Soak the lentils for a few hours. Rinse thoroughly, then add to a large pan of water. Bring to the boil, cover and simmer until tender. Drain well and set aside. Heat 1 tablespoon of oil and gently fry the onion, celery and garlic until softened. Remove from the heat and stir in the lentils, grated nuts and carrot. Add the rest of the loaf ingredients apart from the flaked almonds and mix thoroughly.

Make the filling – heat the oil and fry the onion until softened. Add the grated chestnuts and fry gently whilst stirring for a couple of minutes. Remove from the heat and stir in the cranberry sauce.

Line the base of a 9 inch/23cm loaf tin with greaseproof paper and grease the base and sides of the tin. Sprinkle the flaked almonds over the bottom. Spread half of the loaf mixture into the tin, press down firmly. Spread the filling in next, then finish with the remaining loaf mixture. Again press down firmly and evenly. Cover with foil and bake in a preheated oven at 170°C/325°F/Gas mark 3 for 1 hour. Remove the foil and bake for a further 30 minutes, until golden and firm in the centre. Slide a sharp knife around the edges of the tin and invert onto a serving plate. Carefully remove the greaseproof paper and cut the roast into thick slices to serve.

MUSHROOM, CRANBERRY AND WALNUT BRIOCHE (serves 4)

pastry
8oz / 225g plain wholemeal flour
1¹/₂oz / 40g sunflower margarine, melted
1 egg, beaten
1 sachet easy-blend yeast
1 rounded teaspoon malt extract
2¹/₂ fl.oz / 75ml milk
milk for glazing
poppy seeds

filling
8oz / 225g mushrooms, wiped and thinly sliced

4oz / 100g cranberry sauce
1oz / 25g walnuts, chopped
1 small onion, finely chopped
1 garlic clove, crushed
1 dessertspoon sunflower oil
1 tablespoon natural set yoghurt
1 teaspoon parsley
¹/₂ teaspoon thyme
black pepper

Mix the yeast with the flour. Heat the milk with the malt extract until the malt dissolves and add to the flour together with the melted margarine and the egg. Knead into a ball, then cover and leave in a warm place for 1 hour until doubled in size. Turn out onto a floured board and knead well. Roll out to an oblong of 12 × 10 inches / 30 × 25cm, cover and allow to stand for 30 minutes.

Heat the oil and gently fry the onion and garlic until softened. Add the mushrooms and stir around for 1 minute. Remove from the heat and add the yoghurt, parsley and thyme and season with black pepper.

Spread the cranberry sauce along the centre of the pastry, spoon the mushroom mixture on top and sprinkle with the walnuts. Make diagonal cuts in the pastry sides at ³/₄ inch / 2cm intervals. Plait the pastry strips from alternate sides over the filling to enclose. Carefully transfer the brioche to a greased baking tray and brush the top with milk. Sprinkle with poppy seeds and bake in a preheated oven at 170°C / 325°F / Gas mark 3 for 30-35 minutes until golden.

CHICK PEA, CRANBERRY AND
BRAZIL NUT PIE (serves 4)

6oz/175g puff pastry
6oz/175g cooked chick peas, grated
4oz/100g cranberry sauce
2oz/50g Brazil nuts, grated
2oz/50g carrot, scraped and grated
1 stick of celery, finely chopped
1 small onion, finely chopped
2 garlic cloves, crushed
1 egg, beaten

1 tablespoon sunflower oil
1 teaspoon soy sauce
1 teaspoon parsley
1 teaspoon chervil
1 teaspoon paprika
black pepper
milk
sesame seeds

Heat the oil and gently fry the onion, celery and garlic until softened. Add the carrot and stir around for 1 minute. Remove from the heat and add the chick peas, Brazil nuts, egg, soy sauce, parsley, chervil and paprika and season with black pepper. Mix well and set aside.

Roll out three-quarters of the pastry to fit a lined and greased 8 inch/20cm sandwich tin. Spoon half of the filling mixture evenly over the base. Press down firmly. Spread the cranberry sauce over the filling layer. Top with the remaining filling mixture and press down firmly and evenly.

Roll out the remaining pastry to fit the top. Dampen the pastry edges with milk and place the top in position. Prick all over and press the edges together with a fork. Brush the top with milk and sprinkle with sesame seeds. Cover with foil and bake in a preheated oven at 170°C/325°F/Gas mark 3 for 30 minutes. Uncover and bake for a further 30 minutes until golden.

RAISED VEGETABLE LAYERED PIE (serves 6)

pastry
12oz/350g fine wholemeal self raising
   flour
3¹/₂oz/90g vegetable margarine
4 fl. oz/125ml water
¹/₂ teaspoon mustard powder
¹/₄ teaspoon cayenne pepper
milk
sesame seeds

layer 1
8oz/225g Brussels sprouts, peeled
4oz/100g leek, chopped
1oz/25g Cheddar cheese, grated
¹/₂oz/15g walnuts, chopped
2 tablespoons hot water
1 teaspoon chervil
¹/₄ teaspoon yeast extract
black pepper

layer 2
10oz/300g potato, peeled
2oz/50g frozen cooked chopped spinach,
   thawed
1oz/25g Cheddar cheese, grated
1 rounded teaspoon vegetable margarine
1 tablespoon milk
1 teaspoon chives
black pepper

layer 3
6oz/175g shelled chestnuts, grated
1 small onion, finely chopped
2oz/50g dried dates, chopped
2 tablespoons milk
1 dessertspoon vegetable oil
¹/₄ teaspoon grated nutmeg
black pepper

First make the pastry. Mix the mustard and cayenne pepper with the flour. Place the margarine and water in a small saucepan and heat until the margarine melts. Add to the flour and mix until a soft dough is formed. Knead well on a lightly floured board. Roll out three-quarters of the dough to fit a greased 7 inch/18cm diameter loose-bottomed cake tin. Roll out the remaining pastry into a circle to fit the top. Set aside whilst making the filling.

Now make the layers. Steam the sprouts until just tender, then chop. Add the leek, cheese, walnuts and chervil and season with black pepper. Dissolve the yeast extract in the hot water and pour over this mixture. Mix well and allow to cool.

Chop the potato and boil until tender. Drain and dry off over a low heat. Mash with the margarine. Stir in the spinach, cheese, milk and chives and season with black pepper. Mix well and allow to cool.

Heat the oil for layer number 3 and gently fry the onion until softened. Stir in the chestnuts and cook whilst stirring for a couple of minutes. Take off the heat and stir in the dates, milk and nutmeg and season with black pepper. Mix well and allow to cool.

When all the layers are cool the pie can be assembled. Place layer number 1 in the base of the pie and spread out evenly. Top with layer number 2, then layer number 3. Dampen the top edge of the pastry with milk and place the pastry top in position. Press the edges together using a fork. Prick the top all over with a fork and brush lightly with milk. Sprinkle with sesame seeds and cover with foil. Bake in a preheated oven at 180°C/350°F/Gas mark 4 for 40 minutes. Remove the foil and carefully take the pie out of the tin. Place on a baking sheet and return to the oven for 15 minutes until golden. Allow the pie to stand for a few minutes before cutting.

ACCOMPANYING DISHES

◊ ◊ ◊

TRADITIONAL VEGETABLE ACCOMPANIMENTS

ROAST POTATOES

Allow 8oz/225g potato per person.

Peel the potatoes and cut into even-sized chunks. Heat some vegetable oil in a roasting tin in a preheated oven at 200°C/400°F/Gas mark 6. Par-boil the potatoes for 5 minutes. Drain well and place in the roasting tin. Spoon some oil over the potatoes and cook for about 1 hour until golden. Turn occasionally during cooking to ensure even browning. Drain on kitchen paper and serve.

ROAST PARSNIPS

Allow 6-8oz/175-225g parsnip per person.

Peel the parsnips and cut into even-sized slices. Heat some vegetable oil in a roasting tin in a preheated oven at 200°C/400°F/Gas mark 6. Par-boil the parsnips for 2 minutes. Drain well and place in the roasting tin. Spoon some oil over the parsnips and bake for about 40 minutes until golden. Turn occasionally during cooking to ensure even browning. Drain on kitchen paper and serve.

BRUSSELS SPROUTS WITH CHESTNUTS

Allow 4-6oz/100-175g Brussels sprouts and 2oz/50g peeled frozen chestnuts per person.

Thaw the chestnuts at room temperature for a couple of hours before required. Peel the outer leaves from the sprouts and cut a cross in the base of each. Steam the sprouts with the chestnuts for about 10 minutes until tender.

MIXED VEGETABLE PLATTER

A platter of mixed vegetables makes a very attractive accompaniment. Serve simply garnished with some fresh chopped herbs or with a sauce.

French beans – 4oz/100g per person.
Mangetout – 2-3oz/50-75g per person.
Cauliflower – 4-6oz/100-175g per person.
Broccoli – 4-6oz/100-175g per person.
Carrots – 4oz/100g per person.

POTATO AND SPINACH CASSEROLE (serves 4)

$1^1/_4$lb/550g potatoes, peeled and sliced	1 rounded teaspoon chives
6 fl.oz/175ml milk	$^1/_4$ teaspoon grated nutmeg
3oz/75g frozen cooked chopped spinach, thawed	black pepper
	$1^1/_2$oz/40g Cheddar cheese, grated

Put the potatoes in a saucepan with the milk, spinach, chives and nutmeg. Bring to the boil and cook gently whilst stirring for 5 minutes. Remove from the heat and season with black pepper. Transfer to a casserole dish and sprinkle the grated Cheddar cheese on top. Cover with foil and bake in a preheated oven at 180°C/350°F/Gas mark 4 for 30-35 minutes until tender.

BRUSSELS SPROUTS GRATIN (serves 4)

1lb/450g Brussels sprouts	$^1/_4$ teaspoon yeast extract
2oz/50g Cheddar cheese, grated	black pepper
4 tablespoons hot water	2oz/50g fresh wholemeal breadcrumbs
1 rounded teaspoon chives	1 rounded teaspoon vegetable margarine

Remove the outer leaves from the sprouts. Steam them whole for 10 minutes, then cut into quarters. Melt the margarine over a low heat. Add the breadcrumbs and mix well. Remove from the heat and stir in the Cheddar and chives.

Place half of the sprouts in a casserole dish, season with black pepper. Spread half of the breadcrumb mixture on top. Place the remaining sprouts over the crumb mixture and again season with black pepper. Dissolve the yeast extract in the water and pour over the sprouts. Spread the remaining crumb mixture on top. Cover with foil and bake in a preheated oven at 180°C/350°F/Gas mark 4 for 10 minutes. Remove the foil and bake for a further 10 minutes until crispy on top.

BAKED RED CABBAGE WITH APPLES AND SULTANAS (serves 4)

8oz/225g red cabbage, finely shredded	1 dessertspoon vegetable oil
1 small onion, finely chopped	black pepper
1 large eating apple, peeled, cored and	$^{1}/_{2}$ teaspoon ground allspice
chopped	$^{1}/_{2}$ teaspoon black mustard seeds
2 tablespoons sultanas	$^{1}/_{4}$ teaspoon ground cinnamon
2 tablespoons red wine vinegar	$^{1}/_{4}$ teaspoon caraway seeds

Heat the oil and gently fry the onion and apple until softened. Transfer to a casserole dish. Blanch the cabbage for 2 minutes, then drain and add to the dish together with the rest of the ingredients. Mix thoroughly, cover and bake in a preheated oven at 170°C/325°F/Gas mark 3 for 30 minutes.

PARSNIP AND LEEK CASSEROLE (serves 4)

1lb/450g parsnips, peeled and thinly	4 fl.oz/125ml milk
sliced	1 teaspoon parsley
6oz/175g leek, sliced	black pepper

Put the parsnip and milk in a saucepan and bring to the boil. Simmer gently whilst stirring for a few minutes until the milk is nearly absorbed. Remove from the heat, add the leek and parsley and season with black pepper. Stir well and transfer to a casserole dish. Cover with foil and bake in a preheated oven at 180°C/350°F/Gas mark 4 for about 35 minutes until tender.

CARROT AND CELERIAC IN ORANGE SAUCE (serves 4)

8oz/225g carrot, scraped and diced	$^{1}/_{2}$ teaspoon ground coriander
12oz/350g celeriac, peeled and diced	$^{1}/_{4}$ teaspoon cayenne pepper
6 fl.oz/175ml fresh orange juice	1 tablespoon finely grated orange peel
2 rounded teaspoons arrowroot	

Steam the carrot and celeriac until just tender. Dissolve the arrowroot, coriander and cayenne pepper in the orange juice. Slowly bring to the boil whilst stirring. Simmer for a couple of minutes, then stir in the carrot and celeriac. Continue cooking for a few minutes more. Garnish with the grated orange peel to serve.

SESAME BAKED SWEDE (serves 4)

1¼lb/550g swede, peeled and thinly
  sliced
4 fl.oz/125ml water
1 dessertspoon tahini

½ teaspoon yeast extract
1 rounded dessertspoon sesame seeds
sunflower margarine

Place the water, yeast extract and tahini in a saucepan and heat until the
yeast extract and tahini dissolve. Add the swede slices and simmer for 5
minutes, stirring frequently to prevent sticking. Put half of the swede slices
into a casserole dish. Sprinkle with half of the sesame seeds. Place the rest of
the swede slices on top together with any remaining liquid. Dot the top with
margarine and sprinkle with the rest of the sesame seeds. Cover with foil
and bake in a preheated oven at 180°C/350°F/Gas mark 4 for 30-35
minutes until tender.

FENNEL, CARROT AND COURGETTE
SAUTÉ (serves 4)

4oz/100g fennel bulb
4oz/100g carrot, scraped
4oz/100g courgette
4 spring onions
1 dessertspoon sunflower oil

4 fl.oz/125ml water
½ teaspoon parsley
¼ teaspoon yeast extract
black pepper

Cut all the vegetables into thin strips. Heat the oil and gently fry the
vegetables for a few minutes. Dissolve the yeast extract in the water and add
to the pan together with the parsley. Season with black pepper. Stir well and
bring to the boil. Cover and simmer gently for about 5 minutes until the
vegetables are tender. Shake the pan occasionally to prevent sticking.

MIXED VEGETABLES WITH ALMONDS (serves 4)

1lb/450g prepared vegetables (i.e. broccoli, carrots, mushrooms, courgettes, peppers)	1 teaspoon chives
	1/4 teaspoon yeast extract
	black pepper
1 small onion, sliced	1oz/25g ground almonds
1 celery stick, sliced	1oz/25g flaked almonds, roasted
1 tablespoon sunflower oil	6 fl.oz/175ml milk
8 fl.oz/225ml water	2 dessertspoons cornflour

Cut the vegetables into even-sized pieces. Heat the oil and gently fry the onion and celery until softened. Add the vegetables, water, chives, black pepper and yeast extract and stir well. Bring to the boil, then cover and simmer gently until the vegetables are tender. How long this takes will depend on the vegetables used. Mix the ground almonds and cornflour with the milk and stir until smooth. Add to the pan and stir well. Bring to the boil whilst stirring and continue stirring until the sauce thickens. Stir in half the flaked almonds and transfer to a warmed serving dish. Garnish with the remaining almonds.

CELERIAC AND SWEET POTATO BAKE (serves 4)

12oz/350g celeriac, peeled	1/4 teaspoon cayenne pepper
12oz/350g sweet potato, peeled	1/2 teaspoon ground coriander
1 small onion, finely chopped	pinch of ground cinnamon
4 fl.oz/125ml milk	black pepper

Cut the celeriac and sweet potato into strips. Put in a saucepan with the milk and remaining ingredients. Bring to the boil, then simmer whilst stirring occasionally for 5 minutes. Transfer to a casserole dish. Cover with foil and bake in a preheated oven at 180°C/350°F/Gas mark 4 for 20-25 minutes until tender.

SPICED PARSNIPS WITH ALMONDS (serves 4)

1¼lb/550g parsnips, peeled and diced	1 dessertspoon sunflower oil
1 small onion, finely chopped	1 rounded teaspoon medium Madras
2 rounded tablespoons desiccated	curry powder
coconut	½ teaspoon ground ginger
2 rounded tablespoons ground almonds	½ pint/300ml boiling water
2 tablespoons raisins	roasted flaked almonds

Pour the boiling water onto the coconut and allow to stand for 30 minutes. Put the parsnips in a pan of water, bring to the boil, cover and simmer for 5 minutes. Drain and set aside. Heat the oil and gently fry the onion until tender. Add the curry powder and ginger and fry for a few seconds. Strain the coconut water into the pan and discard the coconut. Add the ground almonds, raisins and parsnips. Stir well and bring to the boil. Cover and simmer gently for 5-8 minutes until tender. Garnish with roasted flaked almonds and serve.

VEGETABLE PURÉES

Vegetable purées make a colourful accompanying dish to go with the main courses. Serve two different purées per meal for 4 people. Choose purées that contrast in colour and serve in a divided vegetable dish.

CARROT AND GINGER PURÉE (serves 4)

1lb/450g carrots, scraped and finely	1 teaspoon chervil
chopped	¼ teaspoon yeast extract
¼oz/7g fresh root ginger, finely chopped	black pepper
4 fl.oz/125ml water	½oz/15g stem ginger
1 teaspoon sunflower oil	

Heat the oil and gently fry the root ginger for a couple of minutes. Add the remaining ingredients except the stem ginger and stir. Bring to the boil, cover and simmer very gently for about 10 minutes until tender. Remove from the heat and blend until smooth. Transfer to an ovenproof serving dish, cover with foil and place in a preheated oven at 180°C/350°F/Gas mark 4 for 10 minutes until heated through. Thinly slice the stem ginger and use to garnish the purée.

PARSNIP AND APPLE PURÉE (serves 4)

12oz/350g parsnip, peeled and chopped	black pepper
12oz/350g cooking apple, peeled and chopped	1 small red eating apple, cored and thinly sliced
1 dessertspoon lemon juice	lemon juice
1/4 teaspoon ground cinnamon	

Put the cooking apple with a dessertspoonful of lemon juice and the cinnamon in a saucepan and cook gently until pulpy. Boil the parsnip in another pan until tender. Drain and dry off over a low heat. Blend with the apple until smooth. Season with black pepper and place in an ovenproof serving dish. Cover with foil and put in a preheated oven at 180°C/350°F/Gas mark 4 for 10 minutes until heated through. Sprinkle the apple slices with lemon juice and use to garnish the purée.

CELERIAC AND SWEDE PURÉE (serves 4)

12oz/350g celeriac, peeled and chopped	1/2 teaspoon ground coriander
12oz/350g swede, peeled and chopped	black pepper
1 dessertspoon sunflower margarine	fresh chopped chives

Boil the celeriac and swede until tender. Drain and blend or mash with the margarine and ground coriander. Season with black pepper and place in an ovenproof serving dish. Cover with foil and put in a preheated oven at 180°C/350°F/Gas mark 4 for 10 minutes until heated through. Garnish with fresh chopped chives to serve.

POTATO AND SPINACH PURÉE (serves 4)

1 1/4lb/550g potatoes, peeled and chopped	1 rounded dessertspoon sunflower margarine
4oz/100g frozen cooked chopped spinach, thawed	1/4 teaspoon grated nutmeg
4 tablespoons milk	black pepper
	fresh parsley sprigs

Boil the potato until tender, then drain and dry off over a low heat. Mash with the margarine until smooth. Stir in the spinach, milk and nutmeg and season with black pepper. Mix thoroughly, then place in an ovenproof serving dish. Cover with foil and put in a preheated oven at 180°C/359°F/Gas mark 4 for 20 minutes until heated through. Garnish with sprigs of fresh parsley to serve.

SWEET POTATO AND ORANGE PURÉE (serves 4)

1¹/₄lb / 550g sweet potato, peeled and
  chopped
1 dessertspoon sunflower margarine
3 tablespoons fresh orange juice

¹/₄ teaspoon ground mace
¹/₄ teaspoon paprika
black pepper
1 tablespoon finely grated orange peel

Boil the potato until tender, then drain and dry off over a low heat. Mash
with the margarine until smooth. Stir in the orange juice, ground mace and
paprika and season with black pepper. Mix thoroughly and place in an
ovenproof serving dish. Cover with foil and put in a preheated oven at
180°C/350°F/Gas mark 4 for 20 minutes until heated through. Garnish
with grated orange peel.

SAUCES

◊   ◊   ◊

Lots of people regard certain sauces as a vital part of a festive meal, the most popular being bread sauce, apple sauce and cranberry sauce. Recipes for these sauces are included, but why not try serving one of the other sauces for a change. The recipes given here have been chosen because they compliment the main courses and can also be served with a plain vegetable accompaniment.

BREAD SAUCE (serves 4)

2oz / 50g fresh wholemeal breadcrumbs
1 onion, sliced
12 fl.oz / 350ml milk
$^1/_{20}$oz / 15g vegetable margarine

6 cloves
$^1/_2$ teaspoon allspice berries
black pepper

Put the onion, cloves, allspice berries and milk in a saucepan. Bring to the boil, cover and simmer gently for 5 minutes. Strain, then return the milk to the saucepan and add the margarine. Stir until the margarine melts. Remove from the heat and add the breadcrumbs. Allow to stand for 20 minutes. Place on a low burner and heat gently whilst stirring before serving.

CHESTNUT SAUCE (serves 4)

2oz / 50g shelled chestnuts, chopped
8 fl.oz / 225ml milk
$^1/_2$ teaspoon cornflour

$^1/_4$ teaspoon grated nutmeg
black pepper

Mix the cornflour and nutmeg with the milk, then liquidise with the chestnuts. Pour into a small saucepan and season with black pepper. Bring to the boil whilst stirring and continue stirring until the sauce thickens.

ONION AND PAPRIKA GRAVY (serves 4)

1 small onion, finely chopped
1 dessertspoon sunflower oil
1 dessertspoon gravy powder
1 dessertspoon paprika
1 teaspoon cornflour

$^1/_2$ teaspoon soy sauce
black pepper
$^1/_4$ pint / 150ml milk
$^1/_4$ pint / 150ml water

Heat the oil and gently fry the onion for about 10 minutes or until soft. Dissolve the gravy powder, paprika and cornflour in the milk and water and add to the pan together with the soy sauce. Season with black pepper. Bring to the boil whilst stirring and simmer gently, still stirring, until the gravy thickens.

MUSHROOM AND BRANDY SAUCE (serves 4)

4oz / 100g mushrooms, wiped and
 chopped
4 spring onions, chopped
1 garlic clove, crushed
6 fl.oz / 175ml water
2 tablespoons brandy

1 dessertspoon sunflower oil
2 rounded teaspoons arrowroot
1 teaspoon parsley
$^1/_4$ teaspoon yeast extract
black pepper

Heat the oil and gently fry the onions and garlic until softened. Add the mushrooms and fry until the juices run. Add the water, parsley and yeast extract and season with black pepper. Bring to the boil, cover and simmer for 5 minutes. Allow to cool slightly, then liquidise until smooth. Return to the cleaned pan. Dissolve the arrowroot in the brandy and add to the mixture. Stir well and bring to the boil. Continue stirring until the sauce thickens.

CARROT AND TAHINI SAUCE (serves 4)

4oz / 100g carrots, scraped and grated
1 dessertspoon sunflower oil
1 dessertspoon tahini
1 teaspoon light soy sauce

2 rounded teaspoons arrowroot
8 fl.oz / 225ml water
1 teaspoon chives
black pepper

Heat the oil and gently fry the carrot for a couple of minutes. Dissolve the arrowroot in the water, stir in the tahini and soy sauce. Add to the pan together with the chives and season with black pepper. Stir thoroughly and bring to the boil. Simmer gently, whilst stirring, until the sauce thickens.

CRANBERRY AND ORANGE SAUCE (serves approx. 8)

6oz/175g fresh cranberries | 2 fl.oz/50ml cider vinegar
1 thin-skinned orange | 2oz/50g demerara sugar

Squeeze the juice from the orange and put it in a small saucepan with the cranberries. Grate the orange peel finely and add to the pan together with the cider vinegar. Stir well, bring to the boil and simmer gently for a few minutes until the cranberries burst. Take off the heat and stir in the sugar. Return to the heat and bring back to the boil. Simmer gently whilst stirring for about 10 minutes until the mixture thickens.

This sauce also makes an attractive gift. In that case allow it to cool slightly, then pour into small sterilised jars, cover and label.

CRANBERRY, APPLE AND PORT SAUCE (serves 4)

8oz/225g fresh cranberries | 4 fl.oz/125ml cider vinegar
12oz/350g cooking apple, peeled and | 2 fl.oz/50ml port
  grated | $^1/_2$ teaspoon ground cinnamon
3oz/75g demerara sugar |

Put the cranberries and vinegar in a saucepan and heat gently until the cranberries burst. Remove from the heat and stir in the sugar. Add the apple, port and cinnamon and stir well. Return to the heat and slowly bring to the boil. Simmer gently until the sauce thickens, stirring frequently to prevent sticking.

This sauce, too, makes a very suitable gift. Allow to cool slightly, then pour into warm sterilised jars, cover and label.

BRAMLEY APPLE AND CLOVE SAUCE (serves 4)

12oz/350g cooking apple, peeled and | 8 cloves
  finely chopped | 1 rounded teaspoon demerara sugar
1 tablespoon fresh apple juice or water | 1 teaspoon lemon juice

Put all the ingredients in a small saucepan. Cook gently until the apple is pulpy. Remove from the heat and discard the cloves. Mash the apple with a fork or the back of a spoon until smooth. Transfer to a bowl and chill before serving.

APRICOT AND GINGER RELISH (serves 4)

8oz/225g fresh apricots, stoned and
  sliced
1 small onion, finely chopped
$^{1}/_{4}$oz/7g fresh root ginger, finely chopped
3 fl.oz/75ml white wine vinegar

1oz/25g demerara sugar
1 teaspoon sunflower oil
$^{1}/_{4}$ teaspoon cayenne pepper
$^{1}/_{4}$ teaspoon ground mace

Heat the oil and gently fry the onion and ginger until softened. Add the
remaining ingredients and bring to the boil. Simmer gently whilst stirring
for about 10 minutes, until the apricots are tender. Serve hot or cold.

DESSERTS

◊ ◊ ◊

CHRISTMAS PUDDING (makes 2 1¼lb / 550g puddings)

Make these puddings up to 8 weeks before needed and store them in the bottom of the refrigerator. To flame the pudding before serving – warm 3 tablespoons of brandy in a small saucepan or ladle. Pour over the hot pudding and quickly set alight before it has time to cool.

4oz/100g raisins
4oz/100g currants
4oz/100g sultanas
6oz/175g cooking apple, peeled and grated
4oz/100g fresh wholemeal breadcrumbs
2oz/50g fine wholemeal self raising flour
2oz/50g dried dates, finely chopped
2oz/50g cut mixed peel

1oz/25g flaked almonds, chopped
1oz/25g dark muscovado sugar
2 fl.oz/50ml sunflower oil
juice and finely grated peel of 1 lemon
1 size 2 egg, beaten
2 tablespoons brandy
1 rounded tablespoon molasses
1 rounded dessertspoon mixed spice

Mix the egg with the molasses, brandy and mixed spice, then add to the remaining ingredients and mix thoroughly. Divide the mixture between 2 ³/₄ pint/450ml pudding basins. Cover the tops with a circle of greaseproof paper, then foil. Tie the tops on securely and steam the puddings for 5 hours. Leave to mature for at least 4 weeks, then steam for 2 hours before use.

CHESTNUT, SULTANA AND BRANDY CHEESECAKE (serves 4)

Chestnuts are used in an unusual way in this recipe to create a crispy base for the rich filling.

base
4oz/100g shelled chestnuts, grated
2oz/50g porridge oats
1½oz/40g sunflower margarine

filling
8oz/225g low-fat soft cheese
3oz/75g sultanas

2 fl.oz/50ml fresh orange juice
2 tablespoons brandy
1 rounded dessertspoon hazelnut and chocolate spread
1 teaspoon agar agar
½oz/15g carob block, grated

Soak the sultanas in the brandy for 2 hours. Melt the margarine over a low heat, then stir in the grated chestnuts and porridge oats. Tip the mixture into a loose-bottomed greased 8 inch/20cm round flan tin and press down firmly and evenly. Bake in a preheated oven at 180°C/350°F/Gas mark 4 for approximately 20 minutes until just beginning to turn golden. Leave in the tin and allow to cool.

Mix the soft cheese with the hazelnut and chocolate spread until smooth. Add the soaked sultanas and any remaining brandy. Dissolve the agar agar in the orange juice and heat until just below boiling point. Add to the cheese mixture and mix thoroughly. Spread evenly over the cooled base and sprinkle the grated carob on the top. Chill for at least 4 hours before serving.

INDIVIDUAL CHRISTMAS TRIFLES (makes 4)

6oz/175g Christmas cake, thinly sliced
4 fl.oz/125ml port
4 fl.oz/125ml water
¾ teaspoon agar agar
2oz/50g stoned dates, sliced
8 fl.oz/225ml milk

2 tablespoons brandy
1 rounded tablespoon custard powder
1 rounded dessertspoon demerara sugar
½oz/15g flaked almonds, roasted
2 glacé cherries, halved

Divide the Christmas cake between 4 sundae glasses. Pour the port and water into a small saucepan, add the agar agar and stir until dissolved. Heat whilst stirring until just below boiling point. Pour over the Christmas cake. Allow to cool, then chill until set. Arrange the sliced dates over the set jelly. Mix the custard powder and sugar with the brandy, add the milk and mix thoroughly. Put this mixture in a small saucepan and bring to the boil whilst stirring. Continue stirring until the custard thickens. Pour it over the dates, allow to cool, then refrigerate for a few hours until cold and set. Sprinkle the flaked almonds on top and place half a glacé cherry on the top of each trifle.

CRANBERRY AND ORANGE TART (serves 5/6)

pastry
3oz/75g fine wholemeal self raising flour
1oz/25g sunflower margarine
fresh orange juice

filling
2oz/50g cranberry sauce
1 orange

topping
2oz/50g fine wholemeal self raising flour
1oz/25g sunflower margarine
1/20z/15g demerara sugar
1 egg, beaten
finely grated peel of 1 orange
1/4 teaspoon ground mace
2 fl.oz/50ml orange flavoured liqueur or
    fresh orange juice
1/20z/15g flaked almonds

First make the pastry base. Rub the margarine into the flour and add enough orange juice to bind. Turn out onto a floured surface and roll out to fit a greased 8 inch/20cm round loose-bottomed flan tin. Prick the base and bake blind for 5 minutes.

Peel the orange and reserve the peel. Finely chop the segments. Cream the margarine with the sugar, then add the beaten egg and beat until smooth. Finely grate the reserved orange peel and add to the mixture. Add the sifted flour and ground mace and liqueur or orange juice and mix thoroughly.

Spread the cranberry sauce over the pastry base and cover with the chopped orange segments. Spoon the sponge mixture over the fruit. Sprinkle the flaked almonds on the top and bake in a preheated oven at 180°C/350°F/Gas mark 4 for 30-40 minutes until golden.

CHRISTMAS PUDDING SUNDAES (serves 4)

8oz/225g cold cooked Christmas
    pudding
14 fl.oz/400ml milk
3 tablespoons sherry
2 rounded tablespoons custard powder
1 tablespoon demerara sugar
1 5oz/150g carton orange flavoured
    yoghurt
1 satsuma, peeled and segmented

Chop the Christmas pudding and divide between 4 tall sundae glasses. Dissolve the custard powder and sugar in the sherry, add the milk and stir well. Transfer to a small saucepan and stir continuously whilst bringing to the boil. Continue stirring until the custard thickens. Pour over the Christmas pudding. Allow to cool, then refrigerate for a few hours until set. Spoon the yoghurt on top and garnish with the satsuma segments.

ICED CHRISTMAS BOMBE (serves 8)

3oz/75g carob block, broken
1¼lb/550g soft vanilla ice cream
1½oz/40g glacé cherries, chopped
1½oz/40g mixed peel
1oz/25g sultanas

1oz/25g stem ginger, finely chopped
1oz/25g walnuts, grated
2 tablespoons sherry
1 tablespoon brandy
1 dessertspoon carob powder

Place the glacé cherries, mixed peel, sultanas, stem ginger, sherry and brandy in a small bowl and stir well. Cover and refrigerate overnight. Melt the carob block in a bowl over a pan of boiling water. Spread over the base and sides of a 1½ pint/900ml freezer proof pudding bowl. Cover and refrigerate until set.

Sift the carob powder into a mixing bowl. Add 8oz/225g of the vanilla ice cream, together with the grated walnuts. Mix thoroughly, then quickly spread over the base and sides of the pudding bowl over the set carob. Cover and freeze for a couple of hours. Put the marinated fruit in a mixing bowl with the remaining vanilla ice cream. Mix quickly, then fill the cavity in the pudding bowl with this mixture. Press down firmly, cover and freeze overnight.

To serve, dip the mould into warm water, then slide a sharp knife around the edge to loosen. Invert onto a serving plate. Leave to stand for 5 minutes before cutting into wedges with a sharp knife.

FESTIVE GARLAND (serves 6)

8oz/225g puff pastry
4oz/100g no-soak ready-to-eat figs
2oz/50g no-soak ready-to-eat apricots
2oz/50g dried dates
2oz/50g sultanas
2oz/50g raisins
1 large orange
1 small cooking apple, peeled, cored and
   chopped

1oz/25g fresh wholemeal breadcrumbs
1 rounded teaspoon vegetable margarine
1 rounded teaspoon ground mixed spice
2 tablespoons brandy
1 tablespoon maple syrup
milk

Chop the figs, apricots and dates and put them in a saucepan with the apple. Peel the orange and chop the segments. Add these to the saucepan together with the brandy and maple syrup. Cook gently until the orange begins to break up, stirring frequently to prevent sticking. Remove from the heat and add the sultanas and raisins. Leave to cool.

Melt the margarine in a small saucepan. Stir in the breadcrumbs and mixed spice. Raise the heat and cook the breadcrumbs for 2 minutes whilst stirring. Remove from the heat and set aside.

Roll the pastry out to a 9 × 19 inch/23 ×48¹/₂cm oblong. Cut off a strip of pastry measuring 1 × 9 inch/2¹/₂ × 23cm and reserve. Spread the fruit mixture evenly over the pastry to within 1 inch/2¹/₂cm of one of the long edges to allow for joining. Sprinkle the breadcrumbs over the fruit. Roll up the pastry like a Swiss roll to enclose the filling.

Transfer the roll to a greased baking sheet and shape into a circle. Pinch the edges together where they join. Lightly roll the reserved pastry strip out and cut out some holly leaf shapes either freehand or with a cocktail cutter. Brush the garland with milk and arrange the pastry holly leaves on the top. Make tiny balls from the remaining pastry and place these in clusters between the leaves to resemble berries. Bake in a preheated oven at 170°C/325°F/Gas mark 3 for 45 minutes until golden.

FIG AND ORANGE PUDDING WITH ORANGE AND BRANDY SAUCE (serves 6)

pudding
8oz/225g ready-to-eat, no-soak figs, finely chopped
4oz/100g fine wholemeal self raising flour
3oz/75g fresh wholemeal breadcrumbs
2oz/50g demerara sugar
2oz/50g sultanas
2oz/50g raisins
3 fl.oz/75ml sunflower oil
juice and finely grated peel of 1 orange

2 tablespoons brandy
1 rounded tablespoon malt extract
1 egg, beaten
1/2 teaspoon ground mace
1/2 teaspoon ground coriander

sauce
8 fl.oz/225ml fresh orange juice
2 fl.oz/50ml brandy
1 dessertspoon demerara sugar
2 rounded teaspoons arrowroot

Put the figs, sultanas, raisins, orange juice and peel, brandy, mace and coriander in a bowl. Stir well, then cover and leave for 1 hour to soak. In another bowl beat the sugar, sunflower oil, malt extract and egg until smooth. Stir in the breadcrumbs, flour and then the soaked fruit. Mix thoroughly. Spoon the mixture into a greased 1 1/2 pint/900ml pudding basin and press down evenly. Cover the top with a circle of greaseproof paper and foil. Tie the top on securely, then steam for 2 hours. Invert onto a serving plate.

Dissolve the arrowroot in the orange juice. Put in a small saucepan with the brandy and sugar. Bring to the boil whilst stirring and continue stirring until the sauce thickens. Serve hot.

MELON WITH LIQUEUR FRUITS (serves 6)

1 ripe honeydew melon
2oz/50g dried dates
2oz/50g glacé cherries

2oz/50g dried apricots
2oz/50g mixed fruit
4 tablespoons fruit flavoured liqueur

Finely chop the dates, cherries and apricots and place in a small bowl with the mixed fruit. Add the liqueur and mix well. Cover and refrigerate for a couple of hours to allow the fruit to soak up the liqueur.

Cut the melon into 6 equal portions and remove the pips. Divide the flesh into cubes but leave these in place, and top each slice of melon with some of the marinated fruit. Cover and chill for 30 minutes before serving.

MINCEMEAT
and recipes using mincemeat

◊ ◊ ◊

Mincemeat is such a traditional food for the Christmas season that the following section is devoted to recipes which contain mincemeat as an ingredient.

Home-made mincemeat is far superior to the shop-bought variety and it is very easy to make. Made according to the recipe given here it will keep for up to 6 weeks once bottled and sealed. It can also be frozen successfully for longer storage. A jar of home-made mincemeat also makes an ideal gift.

MINCEMEAT (makes 4lb / 1.75kg)

1¼lb/550g cooking apples, peeled and grated	juice and finely grated peel of 1 lemon
	juice and finely grated peel of 1 orange
8oz/225g sultanas	2oz/50g demerara sugar
8oz/225g raisins	2 fl.oz/50ml brandy
8oz/225g currants	2 fl.oz/50ml sunflower oil
4oz/100g cut mixed peel	1 dessertspoon ground mixed spice
2oz/50g dried dates, finely chopped	1 dessertspoon ground cinnamon
2oz/50g blanched almonds, grated	1 teaspoon grated nutmeg

Place all the ingredients except the apple and sunflower oil in a large mixing bowl. Stir well, then cover and allow to stand for 24 hours for the flavours to mingle and the fruit to absorb the liquid. Transfer the mixture to a large saucepan and add the apple and sunflower oil. Stir well and simmer gently for 5-10 minutes until the apple softens and combines with the other fruit. Stir frequently to prevent sticking. Transfer to warm sterilised jars, cover and label.

STEAMED MINCEMEAT AND
APPLE PUDDING (serves 4)

8oz/225g mincemeat
1 small cooking apple, peeled, cored and
  grated
4oz/100g fine wholemeal self raising
  flour

2oz/50g fresh wholemeal breadcrumbs
2oz/50g sunflower margarine
1 egg, beaten
1 rounded tablespoon malt extract
1 rounded dessertspoon honey

Cream the margarine with the malt extract. Add the egg and beat until smooth. Stir in the mincemeat, apple, flour and breadcrumbs and mix thoroughly. Lightly grease a 1¹/₂ pint/900ml pudding basin. Spread the honey over the base and sides, spoon the pudding mixture into the basin and press down evenly. Cover with a double thickness of greaseproof paper and a layer of foil. Tie the top on securely, then steam the pudding for 2 hours. Run a sharp knife around the edge and invert onto a plate. Serve hot with custard or yoghurt.

MINCEMEAT AND ALMOND TARTS (makes 15)

pastry
4oz/100g fine wholemeal self raising
  flour
1¹/₂oz/40g sunflower margarine
¹/₂ teaspoon almond essence
water

filling
6oz/175g mincemeat

2oz/50g fine wholemeal self raising flour
1oz/25g ground almonds
1oz/25g sunflower margarine
¹/₂oz/15g demerara sugar
1 egg, beaten
1 tablespoon milk
¹/₂ teaspoon almond essence
15 split almonds

First make the pastry. Rub the margarine into the flour. Add the almond essence and enough water to bind. Turn out onto a floured board, roll out and cut into 15 2¹/₂ inch/6cm circles. Place the circles in greased tart tins.

Cream the margarine with the sugar. Add the egg and almond essence and beat until smooth. Stir in the mincemeat, ground almonds, flour and milk and mix thoroughly. Divide the mixture between the pastry bases. Place a split almond on top of each. Bake in a preheated oven at 180°C/350°F/Gas mark 4 for about 30 minutes until golden. Serve hot or cold.

MINCEMEAT FLAPJACKS (makes 8)

6oz/175g mincemeat
6oz/175g porridge oats

2oz/50g vegetable margarine
1 rounded tablespoon malt extract

Melt the margarine with the malt extract over a low heat. Remove from the heat and stir in the mincemeat and oats. Mix thoroughly, then spread the mixture into a lined and greased 7 inch/18cm square flan tin. Press down firmly and evenly. Bake in a preheated oven at 170°C/325°F/Gas mark 3 for about 25 minutes until golden. Leave in the tin and cut through into 8 equal portions whilst still hot. Allow to cool, then transfer to a wire rack to cool completely.

This is best eaten on the day it is made.

MALTED MINCEMEAT CAKE

1lb/450g mincemeat
9oz/250g fine wholemeal self raising
    flour
2oz/50g demerara sugar

¼ pint/150ml sunflower oil
2 eggs
1 rounded tablespoon malt extract

Put the sunflower oil, eggs, malt extract and sugar in a mixing bowl and whisk until light and airy. Stir in the mincemeat and fold in the sifted flour. Place the mixture in a lined and greased 9 inch/23cm loaf tin. Cover with foil and bake in a preheated oven at 170°C/325°F/Gas mark 3 for 1 hour. Remove the foil and bake for a further 20 minutes until the cake is golden and a skewer comes out clean when inserted in the centre. Allow to cool in the tin for 10 minutes, then slide a sharp knife around the edges to loosen. Turn out onto a wire rack and leave to cool completely.

MINCEMEAT AND CRANBERRY SLICE (serves 6)

pastry
6oz/175g fine wholemeal self raising
  flour
2oz/50g sunflower margarine
2oz/50g low-fat soft cheese
1/2 teaspoon ground mixed spice
approx. 1 dessertspoon cold water

filling
12oz/350g mincemeat
4oz/100g cranberries
4oz/100g marzipan
3 fl.oz/75ml fresh orange juice
1/2oz/15g demerara sugar

Put the flour and mixed spice in a mixing bowl and rub in the margarine. Add the cheese and water and mix until a soft dough is formed. Turn out onto a floured board and roll out to fit a greased loose-bottomed 13½ × 4 inch/34 × 10cm flan tin. Prick the base and bake blind for 5 minutes.

Place the cranberries, orange juice and sugar in a saucepan. Stir and bring to the boil. Simmer until the cranberries burst and the mixture becomes smooth, then stir in the mincemeat. Spread the filling evenly into the pastry flan case. Bake in a preheated oven at 180°C/350°F/Gas mark 4 for 30 minutes.

Roll out the marzipan and cut into 12 stars, using a star-shaped biscuit cutter. Remove the flan from the oven, arrange the marzipan stars on the top and return to the oven for 5-10 minutes until the marzipan begins to brown.

BAKED APPLES FILLED WITH MINCEMEAT (serves 4)

4 medium cooking apples
4oz/100g mincemeat

2 teaspoons honey

Wash and core the apples, cut through the peel all around each apple, and place in a baking dish. Fill each apple with 1oz/25g mincemeat and top with 1/2 teaspoon of honey. Bake in a preheated oven at 180°C/350°F/Gas mark 4 for 25-30 minutes until the apples are just tender.

MINCEMEAT AND MAPLE SAUCE (serves 4)

4oz/100g mincemeat
1/4 pint/150ml fresh apple juice

1 tablespoon maple syrup
1 rounded teaspoon arrowroot

Dissolve the arrowroot in the apple juice. Pour it into a small saucepan and add the maple syrup and mincemeat. Stir well and bring to the boil. Continue stirring until the sauce thickens. Serve hot, poured over a plain pudding or vanilla ice cream.

MINCEMEAT AND VANILLA ICE

8oz/225g soft vanilla ice cream | 6oz/175g mincemeat

Quickly mix the mincemeat with the ice cream until well combined. Spread into a shallow freezer tray, cover and return to the freezer for a few hours before serving.

MALTED FRUIT CHRISTMAS PUDDING (serves 6)

1 12oz/350g malt loaf	1oz/25g demerara sugar
6oz/175g mincemeat	4 fl.oz/125ml cranberry fruit juice
2oz/50g cranberries	2 tablespoons fruit flavoured liqueur
2oz/50g dessert dates, stoned and sliced	2 tablespoons brandy
2 large eating apples, peeled, cored and chopped	$^{1}/_{2}$ teaspoon ground cinnamon
2 satsumas	glacé fruits

Trim the edges from the malt loaf and cut it into 12 equal slices. Place the slices between two sheets of cling film and roll with a rolling pin to flatten. Peel the satsumas and chop the segments. Put these in a large saucepan with the cranberries and 2 fl.oz/50ml of the cranberry juice. Cook until the cranberries burst. Add the apple, mincemeat, dates, cinnamon and sugar and stir well. Cook until the apple is tender, stirring frequently to prevent sticking.

Mix the remaining cranberry juice with the fruit liqueur and brandy and pour into a shallow bowl. Dip the malt bread slices in the juice and use some of them to line a 2 pint/1.15 litre pudding basin. Spoon half the fruit mixture into the lined bowl. Top with a layer of malt bread, place the remaining fruit on top and finish with another layer of malt bread to enclose the filling. Place a saucer small enough to fit inside the rim of the pudding bowl on top and put a 1lb/450g weight on it. Refrigerate for at least 5 hours.

Slide a sharp knife around the edge of the pudding to loosen, then invert onto a serving plate. Garnish with glacé fruits and serve with yoghurt or ice cream.

MINCEMEAT AND MUESLI BAKE (serves 5/6)

8oz/225g mincemeat
4oz/100g fine wholemeal self raising
  flour
2oz/50g muesli base

2oz/50g sunflower margarine
1 rounded tablespoon honey
1 egg, beaten
4 tablespoons fresh fruit juice

Cream the margarine with the honey. Add the egg and beat until smooth. Stir in the mincemeat, flour, muesli base and fruit juice. Mix thoroughly and spread evenly in a lined and greased 7 inch/18cm round flan tin. Bake in a preheated oven at 170°C/325°F/Gas mark 3 for 40-45 minutes until golden. Cut into wedges and serve hot with custard or yoghurt, or allow to go cold and serve as a cake.

MINCEMEAT, MARZIPAN AND
OATMEAL SLICE (serves 6)

5oz/150g medium oatmeal
5oz/150g fine wholemeal self raising
  flour
3oz/75g vegetable margarine
½ teaspoon ground mixed spice

filling
8oz/225g mincemeat
4oz/100g marzipan

Put the margarine in a large saucepan and heat until melted. Remove from the heat and stir in the oatmeal, flour and mixed spice. Press half of this mixture firmly and evenly into a lined and greased 7 inch/18cm square flan tin. Roll out the marzipan to a 7 inch/18cm square and place on top of the crumble mixture. Spread the mincemeat over the marzipan, sprinkle the remaining crumble mixture evenly on the top and press down firmly. Bake in a preheated oven at 180°C/350°F/Gas mark 4 for 30-35 minutes until golden.

This can be served hot or cold as a dessert.

MINCEMEAT, MARZIPAN AND APPLE FLAN (serves 4)

pastry
4oz / 100g fine wholemeal self raising
  flour
1oz / 25g ground almonds
1½oz / 40g sunflower margarine
1 teaspoon almond essence
milk

filling
2oz / 50g marzipan
8oz / 225g mincemeat

topping
1 medium cooking apple, peeled, cored
  and sliced
1 teaspoon honey
½oz / 15g flaked almonds

Mix the ground almonds with the flour and rub in the margarine. Add the almond essence and enough milk to bind. Turn out onto a floured board and roll out to fit a greased loose-bottomed 8 inch / 20cm flan tin. Prick the base and bake blind in a preheated oven at 180°C / 350°F / Gas mark 4 for 5 minutes.

Roll out the marzipan to fit the pastry base. Place the marzipan in the pastry case and spread the mincemeat evenly over it. Arrange the apple slices in a circle around the top and drizzle the honey over them. Sprinkle the flaked almonds on top and bake for about 35 minutes until the apple is tender.

CHRISTMAS FRUIT TART (serves 6)

pastry	*filling*
6oz/175g fine wholemeal self raising flour	6oz/175g mincemeat
3oz/75g vegetable margarine	8oz/225g cooking apple, peeled and chopped
1oz/25g ground almonds	2oz/50g fresh cranberries
½ teaspoon ground cinnamon	1 tablespoon fresh fruit juice
water	1 rounded dessertspoon sugar
milk	

Sift the flour with the cinnamon, then rub in the margarine. Stir in the ground almonds and add enough water to bind. Turn out onto a floured board. Roll just over half the pastry out to fit a lined and greased 8 inch/20cm round flan tin. Prick the base and bake blind for 5 minutes.

Put the apple, cranberries, juice and sugar in a saucepan and cook gently until softened. Remove from the heat and add the mincemeat. Mix well, then spread evenly into the flan case. Roll the other piece of pastry out to fit the top. Dampen the edge of the pastry with milk and press the edges together, using a fork to decorate. Prick the top all over and brush with milk. Bake in a preheated oven at 180°C/350°F/Gas mark 4 for 30-35 minutes until golden.

MINCEMEAT BREAD AND BUTTER PUDDING (serves 4)

The addition of mincemeat gives this favourite pudding a festive flavour.

6 slices wholemeal bread from a large loaf	½ pint/300ml milk
4oz/100g mincemeat	vegetable margarine
1 egg	ground cinnamon

Spread the bread thinly with margarine and cut each slice into 4 triangles. Beat the egg with the milk and the mincemeat. Arrange half of the bread in a shallow, lightly greased casserole dish. Sprinkle lightly with cinnamon. Pour half of the beaten mixture over the bread. Arrange the remaining bread on top, sprinkle lightly with cinnamon and pour the rest of the mixture on top. Cover and allow to stand for 30 minutes so the bread will soak up the liquid. Cover with foil and bake in a preheated oven at 180°C/350°F/Gas mark 4 for 20 minutes. Remove the foil and bake for a further 20-30 minutes until golden and set.

BAKING

◊ ◊ ◊

With all the mouth-watering aromas and flavours, baking for Christmas must be one of the most enjoyable parts of the festive preparations. Tempt your guests with some home-made biscuits or a piece of home-made cake or gateau. They may be surprised to learn that they are eating healthier wholefood alternatives. All the recipes in this section have a lower fat and sugar content than the traditional alternatives. Some of the recipes would also make ideal Christmas gifts.

CAROB LOG

sponge
3 size 2 eggs
2 tablespoons clear honey
2¹/₂oz/65g fine wholemeal self raising
 flour
¹/₂oz/15g carob powder

filling
4oz/100g quark

1 dessertspoon golden icing sugar
1 dessertspoon carob powder
apricot jam

topping
3oz/75g carob block, broken
2 squares of carob block, grated

Whisk the eggs and honey in a large bowl until light and frothy. Fold in the sifted flour and carob powder. Pour the mixture into a lined and greased 13 × 9 inch/33 × 23cm Swiss roll tin and bake in a preheated oven at 180°C/350°F/Gas mark 4 for 8-10 minutes or until the sponge is springy when pressed with a finger. Turn out onto a sheet of greaseproof paper. Gently remove the lining paper. Place another sheet of greaseproof paper on top of the sponge and roll it up loosely with the paper inside. Leave until cold.

Mix the quark with the carob powder and icing sugar until smooth. Unwrap the Swiss roll, removing the paper, and spread evenly with apricot jam. Spread the quark over the jam. Roll up again and place on a plate with the join underneath. Melt the broken carob block in a bowl over a pan of boiling water. Spread evenly over the cake and sprinkle the grated carob on the top. Add a few festive cake decorations and refrigerate until cold. Cut into slices to serve.

Owing to the soft cheese filling this carob log must be stored in the refrigerator.

CHRISTMAS CAKE

8oz/225g fine wholemeal self raising flour
8oz/225g currants
8oz/225g sultanas
8oz/225g raisins
4oz/100g cut mixed peel
4oz/100g glacé cherries, washed, dried and quartered
4oz/100g sunflower margarine
4oz/100g dark muscovado sugar
2oz/50g blanched almonds, chopped

2oz/50g walnuts, chopped
2oz/50g ground almonds
3 size 2 eggs, beaten
3 tablespoons brandy
1 rounded tablespoon molasses
1 teaspoon ground mixed spice
1 teaspoon ground allspice
1 teaspoon ground cinnamon
1/2 teaspoon ground mace
extra brandy

Mix the flour with the currants, sultanas, raisins, mixed peel, cherries, blanched almonds, walnuts, ground almonds and spices. In another large mixing bowl cream the margarine with the sugar and molasses until smooth. Beat in the brandy and eggs and mix again until smooth. Gradually add the flour and fruit mixture and mix to a stiff consistency.

Line an 8 inch/20cm round loose-bottomed cake tin with greaseproof paper and grease. Spoon the cake mixture into the tin, pressing down firmly and evenly. Make a slight well in the centre. Cover with foil and bake in a preheated oven at 150°C/300°F/Gas mark 2 for 2 hours. Uncover and bake for a further 30-45 minutes or until a skewer comes out clean when inserted in the centre of the cake. Allow to cool in the tin, then brush the cake all over with brandy. Wrap in foil, store in a cake tin in a cool dry place and leave to mature for at least 4 weeks.

You might like to leave the cake as it is, or decorate it with nuts. Arrange a selection of mixed shelled nuts on top of the cake. Make a glaze by heating 2 tablespoons of apricot jam with a little water, mixing until smooth, then brushing over the nuts. Alternatively, finish the cake with marzipan. First brush the cake all over with apricot jam, then cover with a thin layer of marzipan. Arrange a few nuts on top and decorate with festive cake decorations and a red ribbon or cake frill tied around the cake.

STOLLEN

8oz/225g plain wholemeal flour
4oz/100g marzipan
2oz/50g sunflower margarine, melted
2oz/50g cut mixed peel
2oz/50g sultanas
2oz/50g raisins
approx. 2½ fl.oz/65ml milk, warmed
2 tablespoons brandy
1 dessertspoon easy-blend yeast

1 teaspoon ground mixed spice
1 egg, beaten
apricot jam

icing
1oz/25g golden icing sugar
1 teaspoon almond essence
2 teaspoons lemon juice

Put the mixed peel, sultanas and raisins in a small bowl and add the brandy. Leave to soak for 30 minutes. Mix the yeast and mixed spice with the flour and stir in the soaked fruit. Add the melted margarine, egg and enough milk to mix into a soft dough. Knead the dough, then place it in a bowl and cover with cling film. Leave in a warm place for 1 hour until it has risen.

Turn the dough out onto a floured board and knead again. Roll it out to a 9 inch/23cm square. Spread lightly with apricot jam. Roll out the marzipan to a 9 × 4 inch/23 × 10cm oblong. Place this along the centre of the dough and fold the two sides of dough towards the centre to enclose the marzipan. Pinch the dough together where it meets and place with the join underneath on a greased baking sheet. Cover and allow to stand in a warm place for 30 minutes. Uncover and bake in a preheated oven at 180°C/350°F/Gas mark 4 for 30 minutes.

Mix the icing sugar with the almond essence and lemon juice until smooth. Drizzle over the top of the stollen. Allow to cool on a wire rack and cut into slices to serve.

CAROB COVERED COCONUT BARS (makes 10)

biscuits
2oz/50g fine wholemeal self raising flour
2oz/50g ground brown rice
2oz/50g desiccated coconut
2oz/50g vegetable margarine
1oz/25g demerara sugar

2 tablespoons milk

topping
2oz/50g carob block, broken
2 tablespoons desiccated coconut

Cream the margarine with the sugar. Work in the flour, ground rice and coconut, then add the milk. Mix thoroughly, then spoon the mixture into a lined and greased 7 inch/18cm square flan tin. Press down firmly and evenly. Cut into 10 equal-sized bars. Bake in a preheated oven at 180°C/350°F/Gas mark 4 for 20-25 minutes until golden.

Melt the carob block in a bowl over a pan of simmering water. Stir in the coconut and spread the mixture over the biscuits. Allow to cool, then separate into bars again.

CHRISTMAS GATEAU

sponge
6oz/175g fine wholemeal self raising
   flour
2oz/50g demerara sugar
2 eggs
¼ pint/150ml sunflower oil
1 rounded tablespoon carob powder
1 rounded teaspoon baking powder
4 tablespoons milk

filling
6oz/175g low-fat soft cheese
1 dessertspoon carob powder
2oz/50g sultanas
2oz/50g raisins
2oz/50g dried dates, finely chopped
2oz/50g cranberry sauce
2 tablespoons brandy

topping
4oz/100g carob block, broken
desiccated coconut
festive cake decorations

Put the sultanas, raisins and dates for the filling in a bowl and pour the brandy over them. Stir well, cover and leave to stand whilst making the sponge. Whisk the eggs with the sugar until light and airy. Add the sunflower oil and milk and stir well. Fold in the sifted flour, baking powder and carob powder. Divide this mixture between 2 lined and greased 8 inch/20cm round sandwich tins. Spread out evenly and indent the centres slightly. Bake in a preheated oven at 180°C/350°F/Gas mark 4 for about 15 minutes until springy in the centres. Turn out onto a wire rack and allow to cool.

When cool cut each sponge in half to make 4 8 inch/20cm circles. Mix the cheese with the dessertspoonful of carob powder until well combined and smooth. Mix the cranberry sauce with the soaked fruit. Place one of the sponge circles on a plate and spread with a third of the soft cheese. Top with a third of the fruit mixture. Repeat these layers twice and finish with the last sponge on the top. Press down lightly.

Melt the carob block in a bowl over a pan of boiling water. Spread the carob over the top and sides of the gateau and sprinkle with desiccated coconut. Refrigerate for a few hours until the carob has set. Decorate with festive cake decorations.

This gateau must be stored in the refrigerator because of its soft cheese filling.

CRANBERRY AND RAISIN BRAN LOAF

This loaf is quick and easy to make and because of the addition of the bran flakes has a lovely chewy texture.

6oz/175g fine wholemeal self raising flour	8 fl.oz/225ml milk
4oz/100g bran flakes	1 egg, beaten
4oz/100g cranberry sauce	1 rounded tablespoon honey
4oz/100g raisins	1 rounded teaspoon baking powder
	1/2 teaspoon ground mixed spice

Place the honey, egg, milk, cranberry sauce and raisins in a mixing bowl and mix thoroughly. Add the bran flakes and sifted flour, baking powder and mixed spice and mix well. Pour the mixture into a lined and greased 8 inch/20cm loaf tin. Level the top and cover loosely with foil. Bake in a preheated oven at 180°C/350°F/Gas mark 4 for 40 minutes. Remove the foil and bake for a further 10 minutes until golden on top and a skewer comes out clean when inserted in the centre. Turn out onto a wire rack and allow to cool. Cut into slices and serve thinly spread with sunflower margarine.

SPICED BRANDY TRAY BAKE (makes 10)

4oz/100g fine wholemeal self raising flour	2oz/50g demerara sugar
2oz/50g cornflour	1 rounded teaspoon ground mixed spice
2oz/50g vegetable margarine	2 tablespoons brandy
	2 tablespoons milk

Mix the cornflour with the sifted flour and ground mixed spice and rub in the margarine. Stir in the sugar and add the brandy and milk. Mix well, then pile into a lined and greased 8 inch/20cm square sandwich tin. Press down firmly and evenly. Make a swirling pattern on the top using a fork. Cut through into 10 equal portions and bake in a preheated oven at 180°C/350°F/Gas mark 4 for about 30 minutes until golden. Allow to cool in the tin, then cut through again to separate the portions.

CHOCOLATE, COCONUT AND CHERRY BITES (makes 24)

2oz/50g fine wholemeal self raising flour	1 egg, beaten
1oz/25g desiccated coconut	4 tablespoons milk
1oz/25g sunflower margarine	12 glacé cherries, halved
1 rounded tablespoon hazelnut and chocolate spread	

Cream the hazelnut and chocolate spread with the margarine. Add the egg and beat until smooth. Stir in the coconut, flour and milk and mix thoroughly. Divide the mixture between 24 petit four cases. Place half a glacé cherry on top of each and bake in a preheated oven at 180°C/350°F/Gas mark 4 for 15-20 minutes. Cool on a wire rack.

PECAN AND DATE BUNS (makes 8)

6oz/175g fine wholemeal self raising flour	¹/₂ teaspoon ground cinnamon
2oz/50g sunflower margarine	1 egg, beaten
2oz/50g pecan nuts, grated	1 tablespoon milk
1oz/25g demerara sugar	2oz/50g dried dates, finely chopped
	2 fl.oz/50ml water

Rub the margarine into the sifted flour and cinnamon. Stir in the nuts and sugar. Add the egg and milk and mix well until a soft dough is formed. Roll the dough into a sausage shape and cut it into 8 equal portions. Roll each portion into a ball and make an indentation in the top of each using a thumb. Flatten each bun slightly and place them on a greased baking tray. Bake in a preheated oven at 180°C/350°F/Gas mark 4 for 10 minutes, then remove from the oven and push in the indentation again. Return to the oven and bake for a further 10 minutes until golden.

Put the dates and water in a small saucepan. Bring to the boil and simmer gently until the mixture becomes thick. Divide the date mixture between the hollows in the buns and allow them to cool on a wire rack.

WALNUT AND CAROB CHIP COOKIES (makes 10)

2oz/50g fine oatmeal	1oz/25g walnuts, grated
2oz/50g fine wholemeal self raising flour	1oz/25g carob chips
2oz/50g vegetable margarine	1 tablespoon milk
1oz/25g demerara sugar	1/2 teaspoon vanilla essence

Cream the margarine with the sugar. Stir in the grated walnuts, carob chips, milk and vanilla essence. Work in the oatmeal and flour until a soft dough is formed. Take dessertspoonfuls of the mixture, and using floured hands, shape into 10 flat rounds. Place on a greased baking tray and bake in a preheated oven at 170°C/325°F/Gas mark 3 for about 10 minutes until golden. Transfer the cookies to a wire rack and allow to cool.

CHRISTMAS STARS (makes approx. 36)

5oz/150g fine wholemeal self raising flour	1 tablespoon honey
	1 rounded teaspoon ground mixed spice
2oz/50g semolina	
2oz/50g sunflower margarine	*topping*
1oz/25g demerara sugar	2oz/50g carob block, broken
1 egg, beaten	18 glacé cherries, halved

Cream the margarine with the sugar and honey. Add the egg and beat until smooth. Work in the sifted flour and mixed spice and the semolina until a soft dough is formed. Turn out onto a floured board and roll out to approximately 1/8 inch/3mm thick. Cut into star shapes using a star-shaped biscuit cutter. Gather up the remaining dough and repeat until it is all used. Arrange the star shapes on a greased baking sheet and bake in a preheated oven at 180°C/350°F/Gas mark 4 for about 10 minutes until golden. Cool on a wire rack.

Place the broken carob in a bowl over a pan of boiling water to melt. Spread the top of each biscuit with a layer of carob and place a halved glacé cherry in the centre of each. Allow the carob to set before serving.

ALMOND SHORTBREAD (makes 10)

4oz/100g fine wholemeal self raising flour	1¹/₂oz/40g ground brown rice
3oz/75g vegetable margarine	1¹/₂oz/40g demerara sugar
2oz/50g ground almonds	1 teaspoon almond essence
1¹/₂oz/40g cornflour	10 split almonds

Mix the flour with the ground almonds, cornflour and ground brown rice. Rub in the margarine until the mixture resembles breadcrumbs. Stir in the sugar and almond essence and mix well. Spoon the mixture into a lined 7 inch/18cm square flan tin and press down firmly and evenly using the back of a spoon. Cut through into 10 equal sections and press a split almond in the centre of each section. Bake in a preheated oven at 180°C/350°F/Gas mark 4 for about 20 minutes until golden. Cut through into sections again and carefully transfer to a wire rack to cool.

PART 2
SEASONS AND
CELEBRATIONS

SHROVE TUESDAY

◊ ◊ ◊

Shrove Tuesday, or Pancake Day as it is often called, can be celebrated by serving a savoury pancake dish for the main course or alternatively by having sweet pancakes as a dessert course.

A selection of savoury pancake recipes is included here, together with ideas for sweet pancakes and fillings.

Pancakes are very easy to make and are ideal casings for sweet or savoury fillings. You will find a non-stick frying pan useful as less oil will be required for cooking and the pancakes will be much easier to toss.

Incidentally, pancakes need not be confined to Shrove Tuesday – they taste just as good on any other day of the year!

BASIC PANCAKE MIXTURE (makes 8)

4oz / 100g plain wholemeal flour
½ pint / 300ml milk

1 egg
vegetable oil

Beat the egg with the milk, then add the flour. Beat thoroughly until smooth and no lumps remain. Brush a 7 inch / 18cm frying pan with a little vegetable oil. Heat until really hot. Pour in a little batter and swirl around the pan to cover the base completely. Cook for a minute or two until the underside turns golden. Loosen the edges with a palette knife and flip or toss over. Cook the other side until golden, then turn out onto a sheet of greaseproof paper. Repeat with the remaining batter until it is all used up. Stack the cooked pancakes on top of each other with a sheet of greaseproof paper in between each. Cover with foil and keep the stack warm in a warm oven until ready to serve.

SPINACH PANCAKES WITH CHEESY MUSHROOM AND LEEK FILLING (serves 4)

1 quantity basic pancake mixture
  (see p.55)
2oz/50g frozen cooked chopped spinach,
  thawed
black pepper
1 teaspoon chives
1/4 teaspoon grated nutmeg

filling
12oz/350g button mushrooms, wiped
  and sliced

8oz/225g leek, trimmed and thinly sliced
1 garlic clove, crushed
1 tablespoon vegetable oil
8 fl.oz/225ml milk
2 rounded dessertspoons cornflour
2oz/50g Cheddar cheese, grated
black pepper
1 rounded teaspoon parsley
1 rounded teaspoon thyme
2 tomatoes, sliced

Mix the spinach with the pancake mixture. Add the chives and nutmeg and season with black pepper. Make 8 7 inch/18cm pancakes with this mixture and keep warm whilst making the filling.

Heat the oil and gently fry the leek and garlic until softened. Add the mushrooms and fry for 3 minutes whilst stirring. Dissolve the cornflour in the milk and add to the pan together with the Cheddar, parsley and thyme, and season with black pepper. Bring to the boil whilst stirring and continue stirring until the sauce thickens. Divide the filling between the 8 pancakes and fold them to enclose the filling. Garnish with the tomato slices to serve.

PEANUT PANCAKES WITH SWEET AND SOUR MUSHROOM FILLING (serves 4)

pancake mixture
4oz/100g plain wholemeal flour
2oz/50g roasted peanuts, finely grated
14 fl.oz/400ml milk
1 egg
1 teaspoon parsley
black pepper
vegetable oil

filling
12oz/350g button mushrooms, wiped and sliced
4oz/100g red pepper, finely sliced
4oz/100g green pepper, finely sliced
1 small onion, finely chopped
4 fl.oz/125ml fresh pineapple juice
3 tablespoons sweet sherry
2 tablespoons light malt vinegar
1 tablespoon vegetable oil
1 dessertspoon soy sauce
1 dessertspoon demerara sugar
2 rounded teaspoons arrowroot
black pepper
lemon wedges

Mix all the ingredients for the pancake mixture together and beat thoroughly. Set aside.

Mix the pineapple juice with the sherry, vinegar and soy sauce. Add the arrowroot and sugar, season with black pepper and mix until smooth. Heat the oil and gently fry the onion and red and green peppers until softened. Add the mushrooms and fry for 2 minutes. Add the sauce mixture and stir continuously whilst bringing to the boil. Continue stirring for 1 minute until the sauce thickens. Keep warm while making the pancakes.

Make 8 pancakes in an 8 inch/20cm frying pan with the pancake mixture. Keep them warm. Divide the filling between the pancakes and fold them over or roll them up to enclose the filling. Serve garnished with lemon wedges.

BUCKWHEAT PANCAKES WITH MIXED VEGETABLE FILLING (serves 4)

pancake mixture
2oz / 50g plain wholemeal flour
2oz / 50g buckwheat flour
1 egg
$^1/_2$ pint / 300ml milk
black pepper
vegetable oil

filling
4oz / 100g carrot, scraped and grated
4oz / 100g courgette, grated
4oz / 100g mushrooms, wiped and finely sliced
2oz / 50g red pepper, finely sliced

1 small onion, finely chopped
2 celery sticks, finely sliced
2 garlic cloves, crushed
4 tablespoons hot water
1 tablespoon vegetable oil
1 teaspoon mixed herbs
1 teaspoon parsley
$^1/_2$ teaspoon paprika
$^1/_2$ teaspoon yeast extract
black pepper

topping
2oz / 50g Cheddar cheese, grated
chives

Heat the oil and gently fry the onion, garlic and celery until softened. Add the other vegetables and stir well. Dissolve the yeast extract in the hot water and add to the pan together with the mixed herbs, parsley and paprika and season with black pepper. Stir well and bring to the boil. Cover and simmer very gently until the vegetables are tender.

Meanwhile, mix all the ingredients for the pancakes together and beat thoroughly until smooth. Make 8 pancakes with the mixture in a 7 inch / 18cm frying pan. Keep them warm.

Divide the filling between the pancakes and roll them up. Place the filled pancakes in an ovenproof dish. Spread the grated cheese on top and garnish with chives. Place the dish under a hot grill until the cheese melts and serve immediately.

SPINACH AND MUSHROOM PANCAKE PIE (serves 4)

1 quantity basic pancake mixture
  (see p.55)
black pepper
1 teaspoon chives
1 teaspoon parsley

filling
8oz/225g frozen cooked chopped
  spinach, thawed
8oz/225g mushrooms, wiped and
  chopped

8oz/225g cottage cheese
1 onion, finely chopped
1 dessertspoon vegetable oil
1 teaspoon marjoram
¼ teaspoon grated nutmeg
black pepper

topping
1oz/25g Cheddar cheese, grated
1 teaspoon chives

Mix the chives and parsley with the basic pancake mixture and season with black pepper. Make 8 pancakes. Squeeze any excess water out of the spinach. Heat the oil and gently fry the onion until softened. Add the mushrooms and fry for 1 minute. Remove from the heat and add the spinach, cottage cheese, marjoram and nutmeg and season with black pepper. Mix well.

Line and grease a 6½ inch/16½cm spring-clip cake tin, or line a soufflé dish of the same size with foil leaving a large overhang of foil to enable the pie to be lifted out. Use 5 pancakes to line the base and sides of the tin. Overlap the pancakes to ensure that there are no gaps and leave the side pancakes overhanging so that they can be folded over to enclose the filling. Spoon a third of the filling into the pancake-lined tin and cover with a pancake. Repeat these layers twice. Fold the overhanging pancakes over to enclose the filling completely. Sprinkle the grated cheese and the chives on top. Cover with foil and bake in a preheated oven at 180°C/350°F/Gas mark 4 for 30 minutes. Lift the pie onto a serving plate and cut into wedges to serve.

BAKED PANCAKE ROLLS (serves 4)

1 quantity basic pancake mixture
  (see p.55)
1 rounded teaspoon chives
black pepper

filling
8oz/225g bean sprouts
4oz/100g carrot, scraped and cut into
  strips
4oz/100g leek, trimmed and cut into
  strips

4oz/100g mushrooms, wiped and sliced
2 sticks of celery, finely shredded
2 garlic cloves, crushed
1/4oz/7g fresh root ginger, finely chopped
1 tablespoon vegetable oil
1 tablespoon sherry
1 dessertspoon soy sauce
1 teaspoon parsley
black pepper
vegetable oil

Mix the chives with the pancake mixture and season with black pepper.
Make 8 7 inch/18cm pancakes and allow them to cool.

Heat the tablespoonful of oil for the filling and gently fry the celery,
garlic and ginger for 2 minutes. Add the remaining filling ingredients and
stir well. Cover and cook for 10 minutes, stirring occasionally to prevent
sticking. Divide the mixture between the pancakes and roll each one up to
enclose the filling. Arrange the filled pancakes in a large shallow greased
casserole dish. Brush the tops with vegetable oil and bake in a preheated
oven at 180°C/350°F/Gas mark 4 for 30 minutes until they are just
beginning to brown and turn crispy.

CHEESY OATMEAL PANCAKES WITH CURLY KALE FILLING (serves 4)

pancake mixture
2oz/50g medium oatmeal
2oz/50g plain wholemeal flour
1oz/25g Cheddar cheese, grated
$1/2$ pint/300ml milk
1 egg
$1/4$ teaspoon cayenne pepper

filling
12oz/350g curly kale
1 onion, finely chopped

2oz/50g Cheddar cheese, grated
$1/2$ pint/300ml milk
$1/20$oz/15g cornflour
1 dessertspoon vegetable oil
1 rounded teaspoon chervil
1 rounded teaspoon chives
$1/2$ teaspoon mustard powder
$1/4$ teaspoon grated nutmeg
black pepper
lemon wedges

Mix the pancake ingredients together and allow to stand for 30 minutes. Make 8 7 inch/18cm pancakes with the mixture and keep them warm whilst making the filling.

Thoroughly wash the curly kale, then chop it and place it in a large saucepan with a small amount of water. Bring to the boil, cover and simmer for a few minutes until tender. Drain and press out as much water as possible.

Heat the oil and gently fry the onion until soft. Mix the cornflour with the milk until smooth and add to the pan together with the cheese, chervil, chives, mustard and nutmeg, and season with black pepper. Bring to the boil whilst stirring and continue stirring until the sauce thickens. Add the curly kale and mix thoroughly.

Divide the filling between the pancakes and fold each one over. Serve garnished with lemon wedges.

DESSERT PANCAKES

Plain pancakes can be served very simply with lemon juice and honey or maple syrup for a delicious dessert. For a change try some flavoured pancakes or for a more substantial dessert add a sweet filling.

FLAVOURINGS FOR DESSERT PANCAKES

The following ingredients can be added to the basic pancake mixture (see p.55) to make flavoured pancakes. Whisk the batter before making each pancake to ensure even distribution of your chosen flavouring.

SPICY PANCAKES
Add 1 teaspoon ground cinnamon or 1 teaspoon ground mixed spice.

FRUITY PANCAKES
Add 2 rounded tablespoons finely grated orange peel or 2 rounded table-spoons finely grated lemon peel.

COCONUT PANCAKES
Use only 3oz/75g flour. *Add* 1oz/25g desiccated coconut. Allow the batter to stand for 30 minutes before using.

CAROB PANCAKES
Use only 3¹/₂oz/85g flour. *Add* ¹/₂oz/15g carob powder.

MOCHA PANCAKES
Use only 3¹/₂oz/85g flour. *Add* ¹/₂oz/15g carob powder, 1 tablespoon decaffeinated coffee granules or powder and ¹/₂ teaspoon vanilla essence.

ALMOND PANCAKES
Use only 3oz/75g flour. *Add* 1oz/25g ground almonds and ¹/₂ teaspoon almond essence.

FILLINGS FOR DESSERT PANCAKES

Each recipe serves 4.

BANANAS AND RAISINS IN MAPLE SYRUP

4 small or 2 large bananas	2 tablespoons maple syrup
2oz/50g raisins	2 tablespoons sherry
4 tablespoons fresh orange juice	

Put the raisins in a saucepan with the sherry and orange juice. Cover and allow to soak for 30 minutes. Peel and slice the bananas and add to the pan together with the maple syrup. Heat gently until warmed through. Strain, and fill the pancakes with the fruit. Pour the juice over the pancakes to serve.

DRIED FRUIT COMPÔTE

8oz/225g dried fruit salad
1/4 pint/150ml fresh fruit juice
1/4 pint/150ml water

1 rounded teaspoon honey
1 2 inch/5cm stick of cinnamon
8 cloves

Wash the fruit thoroughly, then place it in a saucepan. Cover with water and allow to stand for 1 hour. Bring to the boil, cover and simmer for 5 minutes. Drain, then rinse the fruit well with cold water. Return it to the saucepan and add the fruit juice, 1/4 pint/150ml of water, honey, cinnamon stick and cloves. Stir well and bring to the boil. Cover and simmer gently for 30-35 minutes until the fruit is tender. Drain and discard the cinnamon stick and cloves. Remove any stones from the fruit and chop large fruit into smaller pieces. Fill the pancakes and serve with fromage frais or yoghurt.

PEAR AND GINGER

1³/₄lb/800g firm dessert pears, peeled and cored
1oz/25g stem ginger, finely chopped

1 tablespoon lemon juice
2 tablespoons ginger syrup

Slice the pears and place in a saucepan with the remaining ingredients. Cook gently until just tender. Stir frequently to ensure even cooking. Fill the pancakes with the fruit and serve with fromage frais or yoghurt.

SPICED APPLE AND SULTANA

1³/₄lb/800g cooking apples, peeled and cored
2oz/50g sultanas
8 cloves

1 teaspoon ground mixed spice
5 tablespoons fresh apple juice
1 rounded dessertspoon clear honey

Slice the apples and place in a saucepan with the remaining ingredients. Cook gently until the apple is just tender, stirring frequently to ensure even cooking. Remove the cloves and fill the pancakes with the fruit. Serve with fromage frais or yoghurt.

APRICOT AND DATE

6oz/175g dried apricots
3oz/75g dried dates, chopped
12 fl.oz/350ml fresh orange juice

¹/₄ teaspoon ground mace
¹/₄ teaspoon ground cinnamon

Wash the apricots and soak in water for 1 hour. Drain and chop the apricots and put them in a saucepan with the remaining ingredients. Bring to the boil, cover and simmer gently for 30-35 minutes until the mixture becomes quite thick and the apricots are tender. Fill the pancakes with this mixture and serve with fromage frais or yoghurt.

CHERRY AND YOGHURT

1 1lb/450g tin stoned cherries in natural
  juice
2 5oz/150g pots set black cherry
  yoghurt

¹/₄ pint/150ml cherry juice
1 rounded teaspoon arrowroot

Strain the cherries and reserve ¹/₄ pint/150ml of the juice. Cut the cherries in half and mix with the yoghurt. Dissolve the arrowroot in the cherry juice and pour into a small saucepan. Bring to the boil whilst stirring and stir until the sauce thickens. Fold the pancakes into quarters and put some filling in a cavity of each pancake. Pour the sauce over the pancakes to serve.

ORANGE AND SULTANA CRÊPES (serves 4)

8 cinnamon flavoured pancakes
4 orange slices

sauce
2oz/50g sultanas
1 rounded tablespoon grated orange peel

4 fl.oz/125ml fresh orange juice
4 fl.oz/125ml orange flavoured liqueur
1 rounded dessertspoon honey
2 teaspoons arrowroot

Soak the sultanas in the orange liqueur for 1 hour. Use the basic pancake mixture (see p.55) plus ¹/₂ teaspoon ground cinnamon to make the pancakes. Fold each pancake in half, then in half again, and keep warm whilst making the sauce.

Dissolve the arrowroot in the orange juice and pour into a large frying pan together with the soaked sultanas and liqueur, orange peel and honey. Slowly bring to the boil whilst stirring. Continue stirring until the sauce thickens. Add 4 folded pancakes to the pan and cook for 1 minute on each side in the sauce. Repeat with the remaining pancakes. Pour the sauce over the pancakes and garnish with orange slices to serve.

A ST. VALENTINE'S DAY DINNER

◊ ◊ ◊

Create a romantic candlelit meal for two to celebrate St. Valentine's Day. The heart-shaped pies with their rich filling are especially appropriate for this occasion. Lots of the preparation can be done in advance, leaving you to enjoy the meal and not having to spend too much of the evening in the kitchen. Serve the meal with a bottle of your favourite white or rosé wine which has been well chilled.

ST. VALENTINE'S MENU FOR 2
Stuffed baked avocado

Asparagus and mushroom hearts
Piquant potatoes
Mangetout with carrot

Passion fruit and orange delight

Coffee served with lemon and ginger heart cookies (see p.125)

STUFFED BAKED AVOCADO (serves 2)

Make the filling in advance and refrigerate. Cut the avocado just before you want to use it to avoid discolouring. Serve with a light salad garnish.

1 just-ripe avocado pear	¹/₄ teaspoon paprika
1oz/25g cooked chick peas, grated	¹/₄ teaspoon chives
1 dessertspoon cottage cheese	black pepper
1 dessertspoon tahini	extra paprika
1 teaspoon lemon juice	

Cut the avocado pear in half and remove the stone. Mix the ingredients for the filling thoroughly and fill the hollows in the pear with this mixture. Place the stuffed pears in a casserole dish and sprinkle the filling lightly with paprika. Bake in a preheated oven at 170°C/325°F/Gas mark 3 for 20 minutes.

ASPARAGUS AND MUSHROOM HEARTS (serves 2)

The pastry hearts can be made in the morning and refrigerated until needed. Make the filling just before required.

6oz/175g puff pastry	3 spring onions, finely chopped
4oz/100g thin asparagus, trimmed	1 teaspoon olive oil
2oz/50g mushrooms, wiped and finely chopped	$\frac{1}{2}$ teaspoon parsley
	$\frac{1}{4}$ teaspoon French tarragon
4oz/100g ricotta cheese	black pepper

Roll out the pastry just large enough to cut out 4 heart shapes which are approximately $5\frac{1}{4}$ inch/$13\frac{1}{2}$cm at the widest part. Put 2 of the heart shapes onto a greased baking tray. Cut a smaller heart shape from the middle of each of the other 2 pastry hearts, to make heart-shaped 'sides' and smaller 'lids'. Dampen the edges of the hearts on the baking sheet and put the 'sides' on top. Flute the edges of the pastry hearts all around. Loosely arrange the cut out 'lids' in the centres. Make a criss-cross pattern on the tops using a sharp knife, but take care not to cut right through. Leave the pastry to rest for 15 minutes and then bake in a preheated oven at 170°C/325°F/Gas mark 3 for 15 minutes until just golden.

Steam the asparagus until tender. Reserve 4 4 inch/10cm lengths and chop the rest into $\frac{1}{4}$ inch/5mm lengths. Heat the oil and gently fry the spring onions. Add the mushrooms and fry until the juices run. Remove from the heat and stir in the chopped asparagus, ricotta cheese, parsley and tarragon and season with black pepper.

Carefully remove the pastry 'lids' and take out any soft pastry from the insides. Fill the pastry hearts, arrange the reserved asparagus lengths on top of the filling and replace the 'lids'. Cover with foil and return to the oven for 30 minutes.

PIQUANT POTATOES (serves 2)

The sauce can be made in the morning and refrigerated, leaving just the potatoes and celery to prepare.

12 oz/350g potatoes	1 teaspoon tomato purée
6oz/175g tomatoes, skinned and chopped	few drops of tabasco sauce
	pinch of ground bay leaves
1 stick of celery, finely sliced	black pepper
1 garlic clove, crushed	6 green pepper berries, crushed
2 cocktail gherkins, finely chopped	2 tablespoons water
1 teaspoon olive oil	fresh chopped parsley
1 teaspoon lemon juice	

Peel the potatoes and cut into 1 × ¼ inch/2½ × ½cm strips. Put in a pan of water with the celery. Bring to the boil, cover and simmer for 5 minutes. Drain and set aside.

Heat the oil and gently fry the garlic until it begins to brown. Add the remaining ingredients except the potatoes, celery and parsley and cook gently until the tomatoes are pulpy and the sauce thickens. Remove from the heat and stir in the potatoes and celery. Mix well and transfer to a casserole dish. Cover with foil and bake in a preheated oven at 180°C/350°F/Gas mark 4 for about 35 minutes until tender. Garnish with fresh chopped parsley to serve.

MANGETOUT WITH CARROT (serves 2)

This attractive vegetable dish only takes a few minutes to prepare.

4oz/100g mangetout	fresh chopped chives
4oz/100g carrot	

Top and tail the mangetout. Scrape the carrot and slice into thin lengths roughly the same size as the mangetout. Steam the vegetables together for about 8 minutes until just tender. Transfer to a warmed serving dish and garnish with fresh chopped chives.

PASSION FRUIT AND ORANGE DELIGHT (makes 2)

Choose really wrinkled passion fruits as this signifies they are ripe and will have the best flavour. These desserts can be made in the morning and refrigerated. Just spoon the yoghurt on and garnish before serving.

1 large orange
2 passion fruits
1/4 pint / 150ml fresh orange juice
1/2 teaspoon agar agar

1 teaspoon maple syrup
1 5oz / 150g carton orange flavoured
  yoghurt

Peel the orange and grate a small amount of peel for garnish. Finely chop the segments and mix with the flesh and pips from the passion fruits. Strain the juice into a small saucepan and divide the fruit between two glasses.

Add the orange juice to the saucepan together with the agar agar and maple syrup. Stir well until the agar agar dissolves. Heat whilst stirring until just below boiling point. Cool slightly, then pour over the fruit. Allow to cool, cover and refrigerate for a few hours until set. Spoon the yoghurt on top and garnish with the grated orange peel.

AN EASTER TEA

◊ ◊ ◊

To celebrate Easter, why not invite your family or friends for a special afternoon tea. It has long been the custom to serve special cakes, buns and biscuits at this time of year and coupled with that other age-old tradition of afternoon tea you will have a winning combination.

Set the theme for your special tea party by decorating the table with posies of fresh spring flowers tied with yellow ribbons and little Easter decorations such as fluffy chicks, bunnies and Easter eggs.

To cater for all tastes offer your guests a choice of speciality teas, herb teas or lemon tea. If you want to make a more substantial spread add some savoury-filled bridge rolls and sandwiches.

PEANUT CHICKS AND BUNNIES (makes approx. 24)

4oz/100g fine wholemeal self raising flour	2oz/50g smooth peanut butter
2oz/50g semolina	1oz/25g demerara sugar
2oz/50g sunflower margarine	1 egg, beaten
	tiny carob chips or currants for eyes

Cream the margarine with the peanut butter and sugar. Add the egg and beat until smooth. Work in the flour and semolina until a soft dough is formed. Turn out onto a floured board and roll out to about 1/8 inch/3mm thick. Cut out chick and bunny shapes using shaped biscuit cutters and carefully transfer these to a greased baking tray with a palette knife. Gather up the dough and re-roll until it is used up. Press the carob chips or currants into the shapes for eyes. Bake in a preheated oven at 180°C/350°F/Gas mark 4 for 10-12 minutes until golden, transfer to a wire rack and allow to cool.

SIMNEL CAKE

Simnel cakes were originally made to celebrate Mothering Sunday when they were decorated with a flower posy. Nowadays they are generally used to celebrate Easter. The 11 marzipan balls represent the Apostles minus Judas the traitor.

8oz/225g fine wholemeal self raising
  flour
8oz/225g mixed fruit
4oz/100g glacé cherries, washed, dried
  and quartered
4oz/100g cut mixed peel
3oz/75g sunflower margarine
2oz/50g demerara sugar
2 eggs, beaten

1 rounded tablespoon lemon cheese
1 tablespoon sherry
1 teaspoon ground mixed spice
1 teaspoon ground cinnamon
3oz/75g marzipan

topping
apricot jam
12oz/350g marzipan

Cream the margarine with the sugar and lemon cheese. Add the eggs and beat until smooth. Mix the fruit with the flour and spices and add to the margarine and sugar mixture together with the sherry. Mix thoroughly. Spoon half the mixture into a greased loose-bottomed 7 inch/18cm cake tin.

Roll out the 3oz/75g of marzipan to a 7 inch/18cm circle and place this on top of the cake mixture. Press down lightly and spread the remaining cake mixture evenly over it. Cover with foil and bake in a preheated oven at 170°C/325°F/Gas mark 3 for 1 hour. Remove the foil and bake for about 20 minutes more, until golden. Remove the cake from the tin and allow to cool on a wire rack.

When the cake is cool spread all over with apricot jam. Roll out 8oz/225g of the marzipan into a circle big enough to cover the cake completely. Place the marzipan over the cake and gently press together to fit the cake. Divide the remaining marzipan into 11 equal-sized pieces, roll each piece into a ball and space these around the edge of the cake. Place the cake under a hot grill until the marzipan just begins to brown. Allow to cool, then tie a yellow ribbon around the cake and arrange some fluffy yellow chick cake decorations on the top.

HOT CROSS BUNS (makes 16)

8oz/225g plain wholemeal flour
8oz/225g plain unbleached flour
1 sachet easy-blend yeast
2oz/50g demerara sugar
6oz/175g mixed fruit
2oz/50g sunflower margarine, melted
2 eggs, beaten
8 fl.oz/225ml warmed milk
1 rounded dessertspoon ground mixed
  spice

crosses
2oz/50g plain wholemeal flour
1oz/25g sunflower margarine
water

glaze
1 rounded dessertspoon honey
1 tablespoon water

Sift the flours and mixed spice into a bowl. Stir in the yeast, sugar and fruit. Make a well in the centre and add the melted margarine, eggs and milk. Mix until a soft dough is formed. Put the dough in a greased bowl, cover with cling film and leave in a warm place for 1 hour to rise.

Turn the dough out onto a floured board and knead well, then divide it into 16 equal pieces. Roll each piece into a ball and place on a greased baking tray. Cover with cling film and leave in a warm place for 30 minutes.

Meanwhile make the crosses. Rub the margarine into the flour and add enough water to bind. Turn out onto a floured board and roll out thinly. Cut into thin strips and use these to form crosses on the buns. Bake them in a preheated oven at 180°C/350°F/Gas mark 4 for 20 minutes. Heat the honey with the water until runny. Brush the buns with this mixture, then return them to the oven for 5-10 minutes until golden. Cool on a wire rack. Serve split and spread with butter, sunflower margarine or jam.

SPICY CURRANT EASTER COOKIES (makes 24)

5oz/150g fine wholemeal self raising
  flour
2oz/50g sunflower margarine
2oz/50g currants

1oz/25g demerara sugar
1 egg, beaten
1 rounded teaspoon ground mixed spice

Cream the margarine with the sugar, add the eggs and beat until smooth. Stir in the currants and work in the sifted flour and mixed spice until a soft dough is formed. Turn out onto a floured board and roll out to about $1/8$ inch/3mm thick. Cut out 2 inch/5cm rounds using a biscuit cutter. Gather up the remaining dough and re-roll until it is all used. Place the rounds on a lightly greased baking tray and bake in a preheated oven at 180°C/350°F/Gas mark 4 for 10-12 minutes until golden. Transfer to a wire rack and allow to cool.

LITTLE NESTS (makes 10)

Miniature eggs made from marzipan can be used as an alternative to the carob or chocolate eggs.

3oz/75g carob bar, broken
1oz/25g vegetable margarine
1oz/25g desiccated coconut
3 shredded wheat

1 dessertspoon clear honey
miniature foil-wrapped carob or
  chocolate Easter eggs

Crush the shredded wheat until it resembles twigs. Place 10 paper cake cases into holes in a deep muffin tin to support the nests. Put the carob bar, margarine and honey in a saucepan and heat very gently until melted and smooth. Add the shredded wheat and desiccated coconut and mix thoroughly. Divide the mixture between the cake cases and press over the base and sides to resemble nests. Place a couple of miniature eggs in each nest and refrigerate until set.

EASTER MAPLE RING

6oz/175g mixed fruit
4oz/100g fine wholemeal self raising
  flour
2oz/50g medium oatmeal
2oz/50g sunflower margarine
2oz/50g dried dates, chopped

2oz/50g dried apricots, chopped
2oz/50g mixed nuts, grated
1 egg, beaten
1/4 pint/150ml milk
3 tablespoons maple syrup
1/4 teaspoon ground allspice

Cream the margarine with the maple syrup. Add the egg and beat until smooth. Stir in the fruit and nuts, then add the oatmeal, sifted flour and allspice and milk. Mix thoroughly and spoon evenly into a greased and floured 7½ inch/19cm ring mould. Bake in a preheated oven at 170°C/325°F/Gas mark 3 for about 40 minutes until golden. Slide a sharp knife around the edges to loosen, then invert onto a wire rack to cool. When ready to serve, transfer the ring to a serving plate and fill the centre with foil-covered carob or chocolate Easter eggs and fluffy chicks or a flower decoration.

CINNAMON FRUIT AND NUT PLAIT

8oz/225g plain wholemeal flour
4¹/₂oz/125g fruit flavoured yoghurt
2oz/50g glacé cherries, washed, dried
  and quartered
2oz/50g dried dates, chopped
2oz/50g dried apricots, chopped
2oz/50g vegetable margarine, melted

1oz/25g pecan nuts, chopped
2 fl.oz/50ml warmed milk
¹/₂ sachet easy-blend yeast
1 teaspoon ground cinnamon
milk
poppy seeds

Mix the yeast with the sifted flour and cinnamon and stir in the cherries, dates, apricots and pecans. Add the melted margarine, milk and yoghurt and mix to a soft dough. Knead well, then cover and leave in a warm place for 1 hour.

Turn the dough out onto a floured board and knead. Divide it into 3 equal pieces and roll each piece into a 12 inch/30cm sausage shape. Form a plait with the 3 pieces and transfer it to a greased baking sheet. Cover and allow to stand in a warm place for 30 minutes. Brush the plait with milk and sprinkle with poppy seeds. Bake in a preheated oven at 180°C/350°F/Gas mark 4 for about 25 minutes until golden. Allow to cool on a wire rack. Cut into slices and serve either on its own or lightly spread with margarine or fruit spread.

CAROB COVERED COFFEE AND WALNUT CAKE

8oz/225g fine wholemeal self raising
  flour
3oz/75g demerara sugar
2oz/50g walnut halves
¹/₄ pint/150ml sunflower oil
¹/₄ pint/150ml milk
1 rounded tablespoon decaffeinated
  coffee powder
1 egg, beaten

filling
3oz/75g quark
1 rounded dessertspoon demerara sugar
1 dessertspoon decaffeinated coffee
  powder

topping
4oz/100g carob block, broken

Reserve 8 walnut halves for decoration and grate the rest. Put the flour, sugar and grated walnuts in a mixing bowl. Dissolve the coffee powder in the milk and add to the dry ingredients together with the oil and egg. Mix thoroughly, then divide the mixture between 2 lined and greased 7 inch/18cm sandwich tins. Spread out evenly and bake in a preheated oven at 180°C/350°F/Gas mark 4 for about 20 minutes until golden and springy to touch. Turn out onto a wire rack and allow to cool.

Mix the quark with the coffee powder and sugar until smooth and spread evenly over one of the cooled sponges. Place the other sponge on the top. Melt the carob block in a bowl over a pan of simmering water. Spread over the top and sides of the cake. Arrange the reserved walnut halves on top. Refrigerate until the carob sets before serving. Store in the fridge.

A CELEBRATION BUFFET

◊ ◊ ◊

Whether it's for a birthday, christening, anniversary or any other celebration, a buffet spread is an ideal way of catering for large numbers of guests. Pay special attention to the presentation of the food, as first impressions really do count. If a celebration cake has been made use that as a centrepiece and arrange the dishes around it as attractively as possible, bearing in mind the colours, flavours and textures of each dish. Garnish the dishes where appropriate with fresh herbs (left in sprigs or chopped), nuts and seeds (roasted or plain), fruits (sliced), olives (stoned and halved) and hardboiled eggs (sliced or quartered).

Laying on a buffet spread is not simple – but with a little careful planning it can be made a lot easier, with much of the preparation being done in advance of the day of the celebration. Certain dishes such as salads have to be made on the day to ensure their freshness.

It is always difficult to gauge how much food to serve at a buffet, when the exact number of guests is sometimes unknown and you are also trying to allow for their varying appetites! The buffet table can be filled out with bowls of spiced nuts (see p. 130), savoury roasted seeds (see p. 131), chutneys, olives, oatcakes and a selection of different rolls and breads served with a variety of cheeses.

The following buffet menu is intended to provide for approximately 24 people. It comprises various little savoury pastries, a selection of salads and savoury dishes and a choice of 4 desserts.

The notes on preparation are given to help you plan the cooking and hopefully make the celebration go as smoothly as possible.

BUFFET MENU FOR 24

Blue cheese, mushroom and walnut puffs
Cheese and celery tarts
Courgette and pecan filo rolls
Aubergine and stilton squares
Nutty carrot parcels
Ricotta and spinach triangles
Edam and walnut bites
Mushroom and olive paté with savoury
  biscuits
Potted stilton with walnuts
Lentil and orange dip with crudités
French bread with peanut hummous

Cocktail kebabs
Mandarin rice salad
Sweetcorn and pasta salad
Kiwi and tomato salad
Celebration salad
Mixed bean salad
Smoked cheese and brown rice salad

Tropical fruit savarin
Apricot and almond flan
Fresh fruit salad
Date and orange oatmeal slice

PREPARATION NOTES

Blue cheese, mushroom and walnut puffs, cheese and celery tarts, courgette and pecan filo rolls, aubergine and stilton squares, nutty carrot parcels, ricotta and spinach triangles – all these pastries can be made and cooked up to 4 weeks in advance, then frozen. Spread out on baking sheets, cover with foil and reheat in a moderate oven for about 30 minutes to warm through before serving. All pastries can be served hot or cold.

Mushroom and olive paté and potted stilton with walnuts – make the day before and refrigerate. Spread onto savoury biscuits or wholemeal bread or rolls just before serving.

Lentil and orange dip with crudités – make the dip the day before and refrigerate. Prepare the vegetables an hour or two before serving and refrigerate.

Peanut hummous – make the hummous the day before and refrigerate. Spread onto sliced wholemeal French bread just before serving. The French bread can either be bought fresh on the day or bought in advance, sliced and frozen. Thaw at room temperature for an hour or two before required.

Edam and walnut bites and cocktail kebabs – these can be made on the morning of the buffet and refrigerated.

Mixed bean salad – this can be made the day before and refrigerated.

Mandarin rice salad, celebration salad, sweetcorn and pasta salad, kiwi and tomato salad, smoked cheese and brown rice salad – these are all best prepared on the day and refrigerated.

Date and orange oatmeal slice, apricot and almond flan – these can be made the day before and refrigerated.

Tropical fruit savarin – make the savarin the day before and refrigerate. Fill with fruit just before serving.

Fresh fruit salad – this is best made on the day and refrigerated.

As you can see a lot of the preparation can be done in advance, leaving as little as possible to do on the actual celebration day. However, you may have to borrow some fridge space from a friend or neighbour the day before to accommodate some of the dishes.

BLUE CHEESE, MUSHROOM AND WALNUT PUFFS (makes 18)

6oz/175g puff pastry
3oz/75g Danish blue cheese, mashed
2oz/50g mushrooms, wiped and finely chopped
1oz/25g walnuts, grated

1oz/25g fresh wholemeal breadcrumbs
1 small onion, finely chopped
1 egg, beaten
1 teaspoon thyme
black pepper

Mix the cheese with the mushrooms, walnuts, breadcrumbs, onion and thyme and season with black pepper. Add the egg and mix well. Roll out the pastry to an oblong shape measuring 18 × 6 inch/46 × 15cm. Spread the filling evenly over the pastry leaving a 1 inch/2½cm gap along one of the long edges for joining. Dampen the edge with milk and roll up the pastry to enclose the filling. Cut into 18 1 inch/2½cm lengths. Place the rolls well spaced out on a lightly greased baking tray with the joins underneath. Brush with milk and bake in a preheated oven at 170°C/325°F/Gas mark 3 for about 35 minutes until golden. Serve either hot or cold.

CHEESE AND CELERY TARTS (makes 30)

pastry
6oz/175g fine wholemeal self raising
   flour
2oz/50g medium oatmeal
1 teaspoon mustard powder
3oz/75g sunflower margarine
milk

filling
8oz/225g celery, trimmed and finely
   chopped

8 spring onions, finely sliced
8oz/225g cottage cheese
4oz/100g Cheddar cheese, grated
2 eggs, beaten
2 teaspoons chives
1 teaspoon mustard powder
black pepper

garnish
celery leaves

To make the pastry mix the oatmeal and mustard with the flour, then rub in the margarine. Add enough milk to bind and turn out onto a floured board. Roll out thinly and cut into 30 circles using a 2½ inch/6cm pastry cutter. Place the pastry circles in greased tart tins. Prick the bases and bake blind in a preheated oven at 170°C/325°F/Gas mark 3 for 5 minutes.

Mix the filling ingredients well, and divide the filling evenly between the pastry cases. Return to the oven and bake for about 35 minutes until golden. Transfer the tarts to a serving plate and garnish with celery leaves.

COURGETTE AND PECAN FILO ROLLS (makes 16)

32 8 × 5 inch/20 × 13cm sheets of filo
   pastry
olive oil

filling
12oz/350g courgette, grated
4oz/100g pecans, grated
2oz/50g fresh wholemeal breadcrumbs
2oz/50g Cheddar cheese, grated

1 small onion, finely chopped
2 eggs, beaten
1 rounded teaspoon thyme
1 rounded teaspoon parsley
pinch of ground bay leaves
black pepper
sesame seeds and onion seeds

Place all the filling ingredients in a mixing bowl and mix well. Arrange 16 of the filo sheets on a flat surface and brush each sheet lightly with olive oil. Put another sheet of filo pastry on top of each oiled sheet. Divide the filling between the 16 pastry layers and spread it evenly along the centre. Brush the edges with milk. Fold the short edges in, then fold the longer edges over to enclose the filling. Place each roll with the join underneath on a greased baking tray. Brush lightly with olive oil and sprinkle with sesame and onion seeds. Bake in a preheated oven at 180°C/350°F/Gas mark 4 for 25-30 minutes until golden and crispy.

AUBERGINE AND STILTON SQUARES (makes 18)

pastry
6oz/175g fine wholemeal self raising flour
2oz/50g sunflower margarine
1 rounded teaspoon mixed herbs
water

topping
1lb/450g aubergine, finely chopped
4oz/100g blue stilton, mashed

2oz/50g fresh wholemeal breadcrumbs
1 onion, finely chopped
2 tablespoons sunflower oil
2 eggs, beaten
1 rounded teaspoon chervil
1 teaspoon thyme
black pepper
fresh parsley sprigs

Mix the herbs with the flour and rub in the margarine. Add enough water to bind, then turn out onto a floured surface. Divide the dough into 2 and roll each piece into a 7 inch/18cm square. Place into 2 lined and greased 7 inch/18cm square flan tins, prick with a fork and bake blind in a preheated oven at 180°C/350°F/Gas mark 4 for 5 minutes.

Heat the oil and gently fry the aubergine and onion for 10 minutes, stirring frequently to prevent sticking. Remove from the heat and add the remaining ingredients. Mix thoroughly, then spread evenly over the pastry bases. Bake for a further 35-40 minutes until golden and set. Remove from the tin and cut each flan into 9 equal squares. Transfer to a serving plate and garnish with fresh parsley sprigs.

NUTTY CARROT PARCELS (makes 18)

pastry
6oz/175g fine wholemeal self raising
  flour
4oz/100g sunflower seeds, ground
3oz/75g sunflower margarine
milk to mix

1 small onion, finely chopped
2 rounded tablespoons tahini
1 tablespoon sunflower oil
1/2 teaspoon paprika
black pepper
2 teaspoons soy sauce

filling
8oz/225g carrots, scraped and grated
2oz/50g pecans, grated

to finish
2oz/50g sesame seeds

Place the sesame seeds in a bowl and set aside. Mix the flour with the ground sunflower seeds, then rub in the margarine. Add enough milk to bind and turn out onto a floured piece of cling film. Roll out to an oblong shape measuring 18 × 9 inch/46 × 23cm.

Heat the oil and gently fry the onion until softened. Add the grated carrot and fry for 1 minute more, then remove from the heat and add the remaining filling ingredients. Mix thoroughly, then spread evenly over the pastry. Roll the pastry up like a Swiss roll to enclose the filling by pulling up the cling film.

Cut the roll into 18 equal portions, using a sharp knife. Roll each portion into a ball in the palm of the hand and flatten slightly. Press each side lightly in the bowl of sesame seeds to cover. Place on a greased baking sheet and bake in a preheated oven at 180°C/350°F/Gas mark 4 for approximately 40 minutes until golden.

RICOTTA AND SPINACH TRIANGLES (makes 24)

12 12 × 9 inch/30 × 23cm sheets of filo pastry	1 dessertspoon olive oil
1lb/450g ricotta cheese	1 rounded teaspoon parsley
8oz/225g frozen cooked chopped spinach, thawed	1 rounded teaspoon marjoram
4oz/100g fresh wholemeal breadcrumbs	$^1/_2$ teaspoon grated nutmeg
1 onion, finely chopped	black pepper
1 egg, beaten	extra olive oil
	sesame seeds
	6 stoned green olives, sliced

Heat the dessertspoonful of olive oil and fry the onion until softened. Remove from the heat and stir in the ricotta cheese, spinach, breadcrumbs, egg, parsley, marjoram and nutmeg and season with black pepper. Mix well.

Put 2 sheets of filo pastry in a lightly oiled 12 × 9 inch/30 × 23cm baking tin. Brush lightly with olive oil and place another 2 sheets on top. Spread half the filling evenly over the pastry. Arrange 2 sheets of filo on top and brush lightly with olive oil, cover with another 2 sheets. Spread the remaining filling evenly over the pastry. Place 2 more sheets of filo on top and brush lightly with olive oil. Put the last 2 sheets on and brush the top lightly with olive oil. Cut through into 12 3 inch/7$^1/_2$cm squares and cut each square in half to make 24 triangles. Sprinkle with sesame seeds and bake in a preheated oven at 180°C/350°F/Gas mark 4 for 35-40 minutes until golden and crisp. Cut through again and garnish with sliced olives.

EDAM AND WALNUT BITES (makes 32)

8oz/225g Edam cheese, grated	2 teaspoons mixed herbs
8oz/225g quark or cottage cheese, mashed	1 teaspoon mustard powder
4oz/100g walnuts, grated	black pepper
8 spring onions, finely chopped	8 Scottish oatcake biscuits, crushed
2 teaspoons chives	1 teaspoon paprika

Mix the paprika with the crushed oatcakes, place in a shallow bowl and set aside. Mix the remaining ingredients together in another bowl. Take heaped teaspoonfuls of the mixture and roll into ball shapes. Roll the balls in the crushed biscuits until well coated. Put on a plate and cover. Chill for at least a few hours before serving.

MUSHROOM AND OLIVE PATÉ

This rich paté can be used cold as a topping for savoury biscuits or warm as a spread on hot crusty wholemeal bread.

8oz/225g mushrooms, wiped and chopped	1 dessertspoon olive oil
8 stoned green olives, chopped	1 teaspoon thyme
1 small onion, finely chopped	pinch of ground bay leaves
1 garlic clove, crushed	black pepper
	fresh chopped parsley

Heat the oil and gently fry the onion and garlic until soft. Add the mushrooms and fry until the juices just begin to run. Remove from the heat and add the olives, thyme and ground bay leaves. Season with black pepper, then blend until almost smooth. Transfer to a serving bowl and garnish with fresh chopped parsley.

POTTED STILTON WITH WALNUTS

8oz/225g blue stilton, mashed	4 tablespoons white wine
2oz/50g sunflower margarine	2 teaspoons chives
2oz/50g walnuts, grated	black pepper

Mix all the ingredients thoroughly. Transfer to a serving dish and chill before serving. Spread onto wholemeal bread, rolls or savoury biscuits to serve.

PEANUT HUMMOUS

6oz/175g cooked chick peas	2 tablespoons lemon juice
1 rounded tablespoon peanut butter	$1/2$ teaspoon paprika
1 rounded tablespoon tahini	black pepper
2 tablespoons olive oil	

Blend all the ingredients until a thick paste is formed. Transfer to a serving bowl. Spread onto wholemeal bread or rolls to serve. Alternatively, thin with a little water and serve as a dip with crudités and pitta bread.

LENTIL AND ORANGE DIP WITH CRUDITÉS (serves 8)

4oz/100g split red lentils	¹/₂ teaspoon paprika
2 oranges	¹/₄ teaspoon cayenne pepper
1 onion, finely chopped	¹/₂ teaspoon caraway seeds
1 dessertspoon sunflower oil	black pepper
1 teaspoon ground coriander	1¹/₂lb/675g mixed raw vegetables

Peel the oranges and reserve a small amount of peel. Chop the segments. Cook the lentils until tender, then drain. Heat the oil and gently fry the onion until softened. Put the onion, orange segments, lentils and remaining ingredients in a liquidiser and liquidise until smooth. Pour into a serving bowl. Finely grate the piece of reserved orange peel and sprinkle on top of the dip. Chill for a few hours.

Arrange a selection of really fresh vegetables on a serving plate:- broccoli and cauliflower cut into tiny florets; carrots, celery, courgette, cucumber, fennel, red, green, orange and yellow peppers, cut into strips; button mushrooms, baby sweetcorn and radishes, left whole; spring onions, trimmed.

Garnish with quartered cherry tomatoes, olives and fresh herbs.

COCKTAIL KEBABS (makes 16)

These little kebabs are very easy to prepare and prove popular with children as well as adults. You can use plain Cheddar or a variety of cheeses – try smoked Cheddar, Edam and blue cheese.

8oz/225g Cheddar cheese, cubed	16 pineapple chunks
16 dessert dates, stoned	2oz/50g cottage cheese
16 cherry tomatoes	1 dessertspoon fresh chopped chives
16 button mushrooms	black pepper

Mix the cottage cheese with the chives and season with black pepper. Stuff the dates with this filling. Thread the stuffed dates and all the other ingredients onto 6 inch /15cm skewers and arrange them attractively on a serving plate.

MANDARIN RICE SALAD (serves 8)

1 small tin of mandarins in natural juice
6oz/175g long grain brown rice
6oz/175g courgette, chopped
2oz/50g frozen sweetcorn kernels
2oz/50g black grapes, quartered
1oz/25g dried dates, chopped

1oz/25g walnuts, chopped
1oz/25g raisins
$^{1}/_{20}$oz/15g pumpkin seeds
1 teaspoon coriander seeds
1 teaspoon chervil

Cook the rice until just tender, then drain and rinse under cold running water. Drain again and place in a mixing bowl with the grapes, dates, walnuts, raisins, pumpkin seeds, coriander seeds and chervil.

Steam the courgette for 2 minutes and add to the rice. Cook the sweetcorn for a couple of minutes, drain and also add to the rice. Strain the juice from the mandarins and pat the mandarin segments dry with kitchen paper. Add to the rice mixture and mix thoroughly. Transfer to a serving bowl. Cover and chill for a few hours before serving.

SWEETCORN AND PASTA SALAD (serves 8)

8oz/225g sweetcorn kernels, cooked and
  drained
4oz/100g red pepper, chopped
3oz/75g tiny pasta shells (conchiglie)
4 cocktail gherkins, sliced

2 tablespoons white wine vinegar
1 dessertspoon olive oil
1 teaspoon mixed herbs
1 teaspoon poppy seeds
black pepper

Cook the pasta shapes until just tender, then rinse. Drain, put in a bowl with the sweetcorn, red pepper, gherkins, mixed herbs and poppy seeds and season with black pepper. Mix the vinegar with the olive oil and pour over the salad. Toss well and transfer to a serving bowl. Cover and chill before serving.

KIWI AND TOMATO SALAD (serves 8)

4 kiwi fruits
4 firm tomatoes
16 cucumber slices
1 tablespoon white wine vinegar

1 dessertspoon olive oil
1 teaspoon basil
black pepper

Peel the kiwi fruits and slice into rounds, cut each round in half. Cut the tomatoes into thin wedge shapes and mix with the kiwi. Mix the olive oil with the vinegar and basil and season with black pepper. Pour this dressing over the tomatoes and kiwis and toss well. Arrange the cucumber slices around the edge of a serving bowl and pile the tomato and kiwi in the centre. Cover and chill before serving.

CELEBRATION SALAD (serves 16)

1 iceberg lettuce, shredded
1 bunch watercress, trimmed
8oz/225g tomatoes, chopped
8oz/225g red kidney beans
8oz/225g tinned pineapple, chopped and patted dry
4oz/100g sweetcorn kernels
4oz/100g mushrooms, wiped and sliced
4oz/100g radishes, sliced
4oz/100g seedless grapes, halved
4oz/100g cucumber, sliced and cut into triangles
2oz/50g yellow pepper, sliced
2oz/50g red pepper, sliced
2oz/50g green pepper, sliced

2oz/50g carrot, scraped and cut into thin strips
2oz/50g sultanas
1oz/25g pumpkin seeds
12 spring onions, finely sliced
2 celery sticks, finely sliced
few sprigs of fresh parsley

dressing
2 dessertspoons olive oil
2 dessertspoons lemon juice
6 tablespoons white wine vinegar
black pepper
$1/2$ teaspoon fennel seeds
2 teaspoons chives

Arrange the shredded lettuce and watercress in two large shallow serving bowls. Mix all the other salad ingredients together and arrange on top of the lettuce and watercress. Mix the dressing ingredients and pour over the salad. Garnish with parsley. Cover and chill before serving.

MIXED BEAN SALAD (serves 8)

1lb/450g mixed beans, cooked (i.e. black
  eye, red kidney, butter beans and chick
  peas)
4oz/100g broad beans, cooked
4oz/100g cut green beans, cooked
6 spring onions, finely sliced
fresh chives, chopped

dressing
2 tablespoons white wine vinegar
1 dessertspoon olive oil
1 teaspoon Worcester sauce
black pepper
$1/4$ teaspoon mustard powder
pinch of ground bay leaves
$1/2$ teaspoon oregano

Place the beans and spring onions into a mixing bowl. Mix the dressing
ingredients together and pour over the beans. Mix thoroughly and transfer
to a serving bowl. Garnish with fresh chopped chives and chill before
serving.

SMOKED CHEESE AND BROWN RICE SALAD (serves 8)

8oz/225g long grain brown rice
6oz/175g smoked Cheddar cheese,
  grated
4oz/100g fennel bulb, finely chopped
4oz/100g carrot, scraped and grated
1 small onion, finely chopped
2oz/50g raisins

dressing
4 tablespoons white wine vinegar
2 dessertspoons lemon juice
2 dessertspoons olive oil
black pepper
2 teaspoons chives
1 teaspoon French tarragon

Mix all the dressing ingredients together and set aside. Cook the rice until
tender, rinse under cold running water and drain. Place in a mixing bowl
with the remaining salad ingredients, pour the dressing over the salad and
toss together. Transfer to a serving bowl and chill for a couple of hours
before serving.

TROPICAL FRUIT SAVARIN (serves 6)

6oz/175g plain wholewheat flour
2oz/50g sunflower margarine, melted
1oz/25g demerara sugar
1 egg, beaten
½ sachet easy-blend yeast
¼ pint/150ml milk, warmed

syrup
3 tablespoons dark rum or fruit flavoured
   liqueur
3 tablespoons tropical fruit juice
1 dessertspoon honey

filling
1 ripe mango, diced
1 ripe star fruit, sliced
1 kiwi fruit, chopped

Mix the flour with the yeast and sugar. Add the melted margarine, egg and milk. Mix until a thick batter is formed. Pour the mixture into a greased 8 inch/20cm ring mould. Cover and allow to stand in a warm place for 1 hour to rise. Uncover and bake in a preheated oven at 180°C/350°F/Gas mark 4 for about 30 minutes until golden and springy. Loosen the edges with a sharp knife and turn out onto a wire rack. Allow to cool.

Pour the honey, rum and fruit juice into a small pan and heat until the honey dissolves. Place a plate underneath the wire rack under the savarin to catch the syrup. Pour the syrup over the savarin until it all soaks in. Transfer to a serving plate. Cover and chill for a couple of hours. Pile the fruit into the centre to serve.

APRICOT AND ALMOND FLAN (serves 6)

pastry
4oz/100g fine wholemeal self raising
   flour
1oz/25g ground almonds
2oz/50g sunflower margarine
½ teaspoon almond essence
water

filling
8oz/225g dried apricots
8oz/225g quark
1 egg, beaten
4oz/100g marzipan
½oz/15g flaked almonds

Mix the ground almonds with the flour. Rub in the margarine and sprinkle on the almond essence. Add enough water to bind and turn out onto a floured board. Roll out to fit a lined and greased 8 inch/20cm round sandwich tin. Roll out the marzipan to fit the base of the pastry case and place on top of the pastry.

Cook the apricots until tender, then drain and chop. Blend the apricots with the quark and egg until smooth. Spoon evenly into the pastry case. Spread the flaked almonds on the top. Bake in a preheated oven at 170°C/325°F/Gas mark 3 for 40-45 minutes until set. Allow to cool in the tin, then refrigerate until cold.

FRESH FRUIT SALAD (serves 12 to 16)

4lb/1800g prepared fruits (i.e. peeled and stoned, if necessary)
12 fl.oz/350ml fresh fruit juice

8 fl.oz/225ml fruit flavoured liqueur
lemon juice

Cut the larger fruits into pieces, and sprinkle any fruit that might discolour with some lemon juice. Place the fruit in a large serving bowl and pour over the fruit juice and liqueur. Stir well, cover and chill for a couple of hours. Serve topped with yoghurt or fromage frais if wished.

DATE AND ORANGE OATMEAL SLICE (serves 6)

crumble
4oz/100g medium oatmeal
2oz/50g ground brown rice
2oz/50g fine wholemeal self raising flour
2oz/50g vegetable margarine
1oz/25g demerara sugar

filling
4oz/100g dried dates, chopped
1 large orange
2 fl.oz/50ml fresh orange juice
$1/2$ teaspoon ground cinnamon

Peel the orange, chop the segments and put in a saucepan with the dates, orange juice and cinnamon. Cook gently until the mixture becomes quite thick. Set aside.

Melt the margarine over a low heat and stir in the rest of the crumble ingredients. Mix thoroughly until the mixture resembles breadcrumbs. Spread half of the crumble mixture into a lined and greased 7 inch/18cm square sandwich tin. Press down firmly and evenly. Spread the orange and date mixture evenly on top. Cover with the rest of the crumble mixture and again press down firmly and evenly. Bake in a preheated oven at 180°C/350°F/Gas mark 4 for 35-40 minutes until golden. Allow to cool in the tin, then refrigerate until cold. Cut into 6 equal portions and serve topped with yoghurt or fromage frais.

A PICNIC

◊   ◊   ◊

As well as fine weather the other essential ingredient for a special day out in the country or a trip to the seaside is a well-stocked picnic hamper.

The foods chosen for a picnic meal need to be easily transported and airtight plastic containers in various shapes and sizes are ideal for this purpose.

All the recipes for this particular picnic meal can be prepared the day before and stored in the refrigerator overnight. Simply pack the food in a coolbox to transport it to your chosen picnic destination. Remember also to pack those other essential ingredients, plates, cutlery, cups or glasses, corkscrew and a groundsheet for sitting on if necessary.

PICNIC MENU FOR 6

Kidney bean and walnut spread with French bread

Picnic pie with fresh apple and date chutney
Cauliflower and mushroom spiral salad
Pineapple coleslaw
Wheat and corn salad

Summer pudding

Banana and date loaf

KIDNEY BEAN AND WALNUT SPREAD (serves 6)

Cut a French loaf into slices before leaving and pack in plastic food bags to transport.

6oz/175g red kidney beans, cooked
3oz/75g cottage cheese
1¹/₂oz/40g walnuts, grated
1 tablespoon olive oil

1 dessertspoon soy sauce
¹/₂ teaspoon paprika
black pepper

Blend all the ingredients until smooth. Transfer to a lidded container and refrigerate. Spread onto crusty wholemeal French bread to serve.

PICNIC PIE (serves 6)

pastry
6oz/175g fine wholemeal self raising
  flour
2¹/₂oz/65g sunflower margarine
1oz/25g Cheddar cheese, grated
1 rounded tablespoon grated Parmesan
  cheese
1 rounded tablespoon sesame seeds
1 rounded teaspoon chives
¹/₂ teaspoon mustard powder
water

filling
4oz/100g sweetcorn kernels
3oz/75g mixed nuts, ground
3oz/75g carrot, scraped and grated
3oz/75g courgette, grated

2oz/50g Cheddar cheese, grated
1oz sunflower seeds
1 celery stick, finely chopped
1 small onion, finely chopped
2 garlic cloves, crushed
1 egg, beaten
1 tablespoon sunflower oil
1 teaspoon soy sauce
1 teaspoon thyme
1 teaspoon parsley
¹/₂ teaspoon paprika
¹/₄ teaspoon caraway seeds
black pepper
milk
sesame seeds and onion seeds

Rub the margarine into the flour. Stir in the Cheddar, Parmesan, sesame seeds, chives and mustard and add enough water to bind. Turn out onto a floured board. Roll out two thirds of the pastry to fit a greased loose-bottomed 8 inch/20cm sandwich tin. Roll out the remaining pastry into a circle to fit the top.

Heat the oil and gently fry the onion, celery and garlic until softened. Remove from the heat and add the remaining filling ingredients. Mix thoroughly and spoon into the pastry case. Press down firmly and evenly.

Dampen the pastry edges with milk and place the pastry circle on top. Press the edges together using a fork and prick the top all over. Brush the top with milk and sprinkle with the sesame and onion seeds. Cover with foil and bake in a preheated oven at 180°C/350°F/Gas mark 4 for 50 minutes. Uncover and bake for a further 10-15 minutes until golden. Cut into wedge shapes and serve either hot or cold.

CAULIFLOWER AND MUSHROOM SPIRAL SALAD
(serves 6)

4oz/100g cauliflower, cut into small florets
4oz/100g button mushrooms, wiped and sliced
3oz/75g pasta spirals
2oz/50g frozen baby sweetcorn
2oz/50g red pepper, sliced
2oz/50g green pepper, sliced
2 tomatoes, chopped
4 spring onions, sliced

fresh parsley

dressing
1 tablespoon olive oil
4 tablespoons white wine vinegar
1 teaspoon Worcester sauce
1 teaspoon chives
1/2 teaspoon mustard powder
1/4 teaspoon celery seeds
black pepper

Cook the pasta spirals until just tender, drain and rinse well under cold running water. Put in a mixing bowl.

Steam the cauliflower and baby sweetcorn until just tender. Cut the sweetcorn into 1/2 inch/1cm lengths and add to the bowl with the pasta together with the cauliflower and remaining salad ingredients apart from the parsley.

Mix the dressing ingredients and pour over the salad. Toss thoroughly and transfer to a serving bowl. Garnish with fresh parsley and chill for a couple of hours before serving.

PINEAPPLE COLESLAW (serves 6)

8oz/225g white cabbage, finely shredded
4oz/100g pineapple, chopped
2 spring onions, sliced
1oz/25g sultanas
2 rounded tablespoons mayonnaise

2 tablespoons pineapple juice
1 teaspoon yellow mustard seeds
black pepper
crisp lettuce leaves

Place the cabbage, spring onions, sultanas, mustard seeds and two thirds of the pineapple in a mixing bowl and season with black pepper. Mix the mayonnaise with the pineapple juice until smooth. Pour over the salad and combine well. Arrange the lettuce leaves in a serving bowl and pile the coleslaw on top. Garnish with the remaining pineapple. Cover and chill for a couple of hours before serving.

WHEAT AND CORN SALAD (serves 6)

4oz/100g wheatgrain	1 tablespoon light malt vinegar
4oz/100g frozen sweetcorn kernels	2 tablespoons raisins
8 spring onions, finely sliced	¼ teaspoon cayenne pepper
1 dessertspoon light soy sauce	black pepper

Soak the wheatgrain overnight. Rinse well and place in a large saucepan of water. Cook until just tender, about 45 minutes. Drain and put in a mixing bowl. Combine the soy sauce with the vinegar and pour over the wheat whilst it is still warm. Cook the sweetcorn, rinse in cold water, drain and add to the wheatgrain together with the rest of the ingredients. Toss well. Transfer to a serving bowl and chill before serving.

FRESH APPLE AND DATE CHUTNEY

This chutney keeps well for a few days in the refrigerator. Serve as an accompaniment to the picnic pie.

1 large cooking apple, peeled, cored and grated	4 tablespoons light malt vinegar
10 fresh or dessert dates, finely chopped	1 rounded tablespoon demerara sugar
1 small onion, finely chopped	¼ teaspoon ground cinnamon

Place all the ingredients in a saucepan. Bring to the boil and simmer for about 10 minutes whilst stirring, until the mixture becomes thick. Allow to cool, then transfer to a serving bowl. Cover and refrigerate until cold.

SUMMER PUDDING (serves 6)

An ideal pudding for a picnic, as it can be transported in the basin and turned out onto a serving plate just before serving.

8 large slices wholemeal bread, without crusts	4oz/100g blackcurrants
8oz/225g stoned cherries, halved	1oz/25g demerara sugar
8oz/225g strawberries, chopped	4 tablespoons water
4oz/100g raspberries	3 tablespoons fruit flavoured liqueur

Put the cherries and blackcurrants in a saucepan with the water and sugar. Bring to the boil, then simmer until tender. Remove from the heat and stir in the raspberries, strawberries and liqueur. Allow to cool, then strain the juice into a bowl.

Dip the bread slices in the juice and use some of them to line a 2 pint/1.15 litre pudding basin. Spoon half the fruit mixture into the basin and top with a layer of bread dipped in juice. Spread the remaining fruit in the basin and cover with another layer of bread dipped in juice.

Place a saucer that is small enough to fit inside the rim of the pudding basin on top and put a 1lb/450g weight on it. Cover and refrigerate overnight. Slide a sharp knife around the edge to loosen and invert onto a plate. Serve topped with yoghurt or fromage frais.

BANANA AND DATE LOAF

6oz/175g fine wholemeal self raising flour	1oz/25g demerara sugar
4oz/100g dried bananas, finely sliced	1 egg, beaten
2oz/50g dried dates, finely chopped	6 fl.oz/175ml milk
1oz/25g sunflower margarine	3 fl.oz/75ml fresh orange juice
	sesame seeds

Put the bananas and milk in a saucepan. Bring to the boil and simmer until the bananas are pulpy and the mixture thickens, stirring frequently to prevent sticking. Cream the margarine with the sugar, then stir in the banana mixture. Add the dates, egg and orange juice and finally the flour. Mix thoroughly, then spoon the mixture evenly into a lined and greased 8 inch/20cm loaf tin. Sprinkle the top with sesame seeds. Bake in a preheated oven at 180°C/350°F/Gas mark 4 for 45-50 minutes until firm in the centre. Cool on a wire rack, cut into slices, spread thinly with butter or margarine before leaving and pack in an airtight container. Serve with tea or coffee from a flask as a snack in the afternoon.

A SUMMER BARBECUE

◊   ◊   ◊

Eating al fresco on a warm summer evening is a pleasant way of entertaining and with a little advance planning a barbecue can be a great success.

A lot of the following recipes can be prepared in advance. For example, the ingredients for the kebabs are best left to marinate for a couple of hours to allow them to absorb the flavours and burgers actually benefit from being made up and then chilled before cooking.

Here are three suggested menus for different barbecue meals, although obviously you might prefer to juggle with the recipes and create your own.

LUNCH FOR 4

Mushroom and courgette saté with
  plain rice
Stuffed tomato lillies
Herb baked sweetcorn
Garlic bread
Maple baked bananas

DINNER FOR 8

Vegetable kebabs with saffron fruit
  and nut rice or jacket potatoes
  with savoury filling
Sweetcorn and pepper relish
Avocado salad
Herby olive oil and onion bread
Spicy fruit and coconut kebabs or
  maple baked bananas

CHILDREN'S PARTY FOR 8

A barbecue in the garden for a few friends might appeal to slightly older children if their birthday falls within the summer months. Make sure that an adult is in charge of the barbecue at all times.

Peanut and cheese burgers
Smoky chick pea and pecan patties
Barbecue sauce
Herb baked sweetcorn
Jacket potatoes with crunchy peanut
  filling
French bread
Spicy fruit and coconut kebabs or
  maple baked bananas

SMOKY CHICK PEA AND PECAN PATTIES (makes 10)

6oz/175g cooked chick peas, grated	1 dessertspoon tahini
2oz/50g pecan nuts, grated	1 teaspoon soy sauce
2oz/50g smoked Cheddar cheese, grated	1 teaspoon parsley
2oz/50g fresh wholemeal breadcrumbs	1 teaspoon ground coriander
2oz/50g carrot, scraped and grated	$1/_8$ teaspoon cayenne pepper
1 small onion, finely chopped	black pepper
1 dessertspoon sunflower oil	extra sunflower oil
1 egg, beaten	

Heat the oil and gently fry the onion and carrot until softened. Remove from the heat and add the remaining ingredients. Mix thoroughly until the mixture binds together. Divide it into 10 equal pieces and shape each piece into a flat round. Chill for a couple of hours.

Arrange the patties on a lightly oiled baking sheet and brush the tops with oil. Place the baking sheet on the barbecue grill and cook for 15-20 minutes, turning once. Serve with sweetcorn and pepper relish.

PEANUT AND CHEESE BURGERS (makes 8)

6oz/175g shelled peanuts, ground	1 dessertspoon soy sauce
2oz/50g Cheddar cheese, grated	1 teaspoon parsley
2oz/50g fresh wholemeal breadcrumbs	1 teaspoon thyme
1 small onion, very finely chopped	black pepper
1 egg, beaten	wheatgerm
1 tablespoon peanut butter	sunflower oil

Put the peanuts, cheese, breadcrumbs, onion, parsley and thyme in a mixing bowl and season with black pepper. Add the egg, peanut butter and soy sauce and mix thoroughly until the mixture binds together. Divide it into 8 equal portions and roll each piece into a ball. Flatten each ball and roll in wheatgerm. Chill for a couple of hours.

Lightly oil a baking sheet with sunflower oil and place the burgers on it. Brush the tops of the burgers with oil and place the baking sheet on the barbecue grill. Cook the burgers for 15-20 minutes, turning once. Serve with barbecue sauce.

HERB BAKED SWEETCORN (for 1)

1 fresh corn-on-the-cob	sunflower margarine
2 sprigs of fresh herbs	

Remove the husks and silken strands from the sweetcorn. Lightly grease a sheet of foil with sunflower margarine. Wrap the cob with the 2 sprigs of herbs tightly in the foil and cook for 15-20 minutes on the barbecue until tender. Turn occasionally.

STUFFED TOMATO LILLIES (serves 4)

2 large firm tomatoes, each weighing approx. 8oz/225g	2 spring onions, finely sliced
1oz/25g hazelnuts, grated	1 teaspoon olive oil
1oz/25g Cheddar cheese, grated	$^1/_2$ teaspoon oregano
1oz/25g fresh wholemeal breadcrumbs	$^1/_2$ teaspoon parsley
1 garlic clove, crushed	black pepper
	fresh chives, chopped

Cut the tomatoes in half in a zig zag pattern to make 2 lillies from each. Remove the insides of the tomatoes and turn the shells upside down to drain. Chop the tomato flesh and place it in a sieve to drain off the juice.

Heat the oil and gently fry the spring onions and garlic until softened. Turn up the heat and add the breadcrumbs. Fry for 2 minutes whilst stirring. Remove from the heat and add the chopped tomato and remaining ingredients. Divide the filling between the 4 tomato shells and sprinkle the tops with chives. Wrap the tomatoes individually in foil and cook on the barbecue for about 10 minutes until just tender.

MUSHROOM AND COURGETTE SATÉ (serves 4)

kebabs
8oz/225g courgette, thickly sliced
8oz/225g button mushrooms

marinade
2 garlic cloves, crushed
2 tablespoons medium sherry
1 dessertspoon soy sauce
1 tablespoon sunflower oil
black pepper

sauce
1 onion, finely chopped
¼oz/7g fresh root ginger, finely chopped
6 fl.oz/175ml water
2 rounded tablespoons peanut butter
1 dessertspoon lemon juice
1 dessertspoon sunflower oil
black pepper
pinch of chilli powder

Mix the ingredients for the marinade together. Place the courgettes and mushrooms in a bowl and pour the marinade over. Toss well and leave to stand for a couple of hours to allow the vegetables to absorb the flavours.

Heat the oil for the sauce and gently fry the onion and ginger until softened. Add the remaining sauce ingredients, then liquidise until smooth. Thread the vegetables onto small skewers and place these on the barbecue grill. Cook for 10-15 minutes until tender, turning occasionally. Reheat the sauce whilst stirring. Serve the kebabs with the sauce on a bed of plain rice, allowing 2oz/50g long grain rice per person.

SPICY FRUIT AND COCONUT KEBABS (serves 4)

1lb/450g mixed fruits (i.e. peach, plum, pineapple, banana)
2oz/50g desiccated coconut

1 rounded teaspoon ground mixed spice
4 tablespoons fresh fruit juice
1 dessertspoon clear honey

Skin and remove the stones from the peaches and plums. Cut the plums in half and cut the peach into large chunks. Thickly slice the banana and pineapple. Mix the coconut with the mixed spice and put in a bowl. Pour the fruit juice and honey into another bowl and stir until the honey dissolves. Dip the fruit pieces into the juice and then into the coconut mixture and stir around until coated all over with coconut. Thread the fruit onto 8 small skewers and cook on the barbecue grill for 5-10 minutes, turning occasionally, until golden.

Serve with fromage frais or yoghurt.

BARBECUE SAUCE (serves 4)

8oz/225g tomatoes, skinned and
  chopped
1 small onion, finely chopped
2 garlic cloves, crushed
4 fl.oz/125ml water
1 tablespoon light malt vinegar

1 tablespoon lemon juice
1 dessertspoon sunflower oil
1 dessertspoon tomato purée
1 teaspoon mixed herbs
$1/4$ teaspoon cayenne pepper
black pepper

Heat the oil and gently fry the onion and garlic until softened. Add the remaining ingredients and stir well. Bring to the boil, cover and simmer gently for 15 minutes.

SWEETCORN AND PEPPER RELISH (serves 8)

This relish can be made the day before and stored in the refrigerator.

6oz/175g frozen sweetcorn kernels
1 small onion, finely chopped
1 tomato, skinned and chopped
2oz/50g red pepper, chopped
2oz/50g green pepper, chopped
4 fl.oz/150ml white wine vinegar

1 rounded dessertspoon demerara sugar
1 teaspoon Worcester sauce
$1/4$ teaspoon fennel seeds
$1/4$ teaspoon celery seeds
black pepper

Put all the ingredients in a saucepan. Stir until the sugar dissolves. Bring to the boil and simmer uncovered for 10-15 minutes until all liquid has been absorbed, stirring frequently to prevent sticking. Allow to cool, then transfer to a serving dish. Cover and refrigerate until required.

HERBY OLIVE OIL AND ONION BREAD

This bread is delicious served warm with garlic or herb butter.

12oz/350g plain wholemeal flour
1 small onion, very finely chopped
$1/2$ sachet easy-blend yeast

2 tablespoons fresh chopped mixed herbs
2 fl.oz/50ml olive oil
6 fl.oz/175ml warm water

Put the flour in a mixing bowl with the yeast, mixed herbs and onion. Stir well, add the olive oil and water and mix until a soft dough is formed. Knead well on a floured surface, return to the mixing bowl, cover and leave to prove in a warm place for 1 hour.

Knead the dough again and shape it into a 7 inch/18cm circle. Place on a greased baking sheet and allow to stand in a warm place for 30 minutes. Bake in a preheated oven at 180°C/350°F/Gas mark 4 for 25-30 minutes until golden. Cool on a wire rack and cut into slices to serve.

VEGETABLE KEBABS (serves 4 or 8)

Serve either 1 or 2 kebabs per person depending on what is being served with them.

2 sweetcorns, cut into 1 inch/2½cm lengths	*marinade*
2 tomatoes, quartered	1 tablespoon olive oil
1 onion, cut into chunks	1 tablespoon medium sherry
8oz/225g courgette, thickly sliced	1 tablespoon lemon juice
4oz/100g mushrooms	1 dessertspoon soy sauce
2oz/50g fennel bulb, sliced	2 garlic cloves, crushed
2oz/50g red pepper, cut into chunks	black pepper
2oz/50g yellow pepper, cut into chunks	½ teaspoon mustard powder
16 bay leaves	½ teaspoon celery seeds

Mix all the marinade ingredients together. Place the prepared vegetables into a bowl and pour the marinade over them. Cover and allow to stand for a couple of hours to enable them to absorb the flavours. Stir occasionally to coat all sides.

Thread the vegetables and bay leaves onto 8 12 inch/30cm skewers. Place on the barbecue grill and baste with the remaining marinade. Cook for 10-15 minutes until tender, turning occasionally to ensure even cooking. Serve with saffron fruit and nut rice.

SAFFRON FRUIT AND NUT RICE (serves 4)

8oz/225g brown basmati rice	few strands of saffron
1 onion, finely chopped	1oz/25g cashew nuts, halved and lightly roasted
1 tablespoon sunflower oil	1oz/25g flaked almonds, lightly roasted
1 tablespoon raisins	1 pint/600ml water
1 tablespoon sultanas	

Heat the oil and gently fry the onion until softened. Add the rice and fry for a couple of minutes whilst stirring. Add the raisins, sultanas, saffron and water and stir well. Bring to the boil, cover and simmer very gently until the liquid has been absorbed and the rice is tender. Remove from the heat and stir in the cashews and almonds. Transfer to a warmed serving dish.

AVOCADO SALAD (serves 8)

This salad can be made in advance, but add the avocado at the last moment to prevent discolouration.

1 large or 2 small just ripe avocado pears, diced
1 crisp lettuce, shredded
2 inch/5cm length of cucumber, sliced and cut into triangles
$^1/_2$ bunch of watercress, chopped
few sprigs of fresh parsley, chopped
6 spring onions, finely sliced

2oz/50g red pepper, sliced
2oz/50g green pepper, sliced
lemon juice
4 gherkins, finely sliced
1oz/25g raisins
$^1/_{20}$oz/15g pumpkin seeds
1 teaspoon chives
black pepper

Sprinkle the diced avocado with lemon juice, then put in a bowl with the remaining ingredients and season with black pepper. Toss well and transfer to a serving bowl.

JACKET POTATOES WITH FILLINGS

1 medium-sized potato per person (weighing approx. 8oz/225g)

sunflower oil

Scrub the potatoes and brush lightly with sunflower oil. Wrap individually in foil. Cook for 50-60 minutes on the barbecue until tender, turning occasionally to ensure that they cook evenly. Serve simply with vegetable margarine or grated Cheddar cheese seasoned with black pepper or alternatively add one of the following fillings.

AVOCADO AND RICOTTA FILLING (serves 4)

1 small ripe avocado pear, mashed
4oz/100g ricotta cheese

$^1/_2$ teaspoon chives
black pepper

Mix all the ingredients together until well combined.

CRUNCHY PEANUT FILLING (serves 4)

2oz/50g fromage frais	black pepper
2oz/50g crunchy peanut butter	1oz/25g dry roasted peanuts, finely
2 tablespoons milk	chopped

Mix the fromage frais with the peanut butter and milk until smooth. Season with black pepper. Sprinkle the chopped peanuts on top of each filled potato.

BLUE CHEESE AND WALNUT FILLING (serves 4)

2oz/50g Danish blue cheese, mashed	1/2 teaspoon parsley
2oz/50g cottage cheese	black pepper
1oz/25g walnuts, grated	4 walnut halves

Mix the blue cheese with the cottage cheese, grated walnuts and parsley and season with black pepper. Top the potatoes with this mixture and garnish each with a walnut half.

MAPLE BAKED BANANAS WITH RAISINS (serves 4)

4 bananas, peeled	1 tablespoon sherry or fresh fruit juice
2oz/50g raisins	4 dessertspoons maple syrup
1oz/25g flaked almonds	lemon juice

Soak the raisins in the sherry or fruit juice for 30 minutes. Split the bananas in half lengthways and put each banana on a sheet of foil. Sprinkle them with lemon juice. Pack the raisins in between the banana halves and drizzle 1 dessertspoonful of maple syrup over each one. Sprinkle with flaked almonds and wrap in the foil. Place on the barbecue grill for approximately 10 minutes until tender. Serve with yoghurt or fromage frais.

A HALLOWE'EN PARTY

◊   ◊   ◊

At a Hallowe'en dinner party the preparation can be almost as much fun as the party itself. Great fun can be had by making up ghoulish names for the food and with a little imagination and some coloured card suitable table decorations can be made to set the scene.

The menu for the party can be stuck onto a piece of black card cut into the shape of a witches' hat. Name plates for the food can be stuck onto cards cut into the shapes of spiders, bats, cats and pumpkins.

Greet your guests with a warming bowl of pumpkin and orange soup served from a cauldron. A cauldron effect can be easily given to a serving bowl with some black, orange and red card. Fold a piece of black card into a tube shape large enough to fit around the bowl. Stick some shaped red and orange card at the base to imitate flames licking up the sides.

No Hallowe'en party is complete without a pumpkin lamp. Use a largish pumpkin and slice off the top to make the lid. Scoop out the flesh and use this to make the soup. Cut out triangles for eyes and nose and a zigzag shape for the mouth. Place a short candle inside, light it and replace the lid. Use the pumpkin as a centrepiece for the table.

The following meal is intended to be served as a sit-down buffet with the soup being ladled into individual bowls at the table and the main courses being presented on serving plates for the guests to help themselves. The reason for this is that some of the Hallowe'en food creates more of an impact when there is a plateful of it rather than a single item sitting on a plate.

HALLOWE'EN DINNER PARTY MENU FOR 8

A cauldron of pumpkin and orange soup served with spellbinding stars

Witches' fingers served with vampire dip
Stuffed wizards' hats
Devilled potato bugs
Spooky sweet and sour beetroot
Magic stones salad
Ghouls' eyes
Demon cocktail bites

Black sundaes

A CAULDRON OF PUMPKIN AND ORANGE SOUP (serves 8)

This soup can be made on the morning of the party and reheated when required. Serve the soup with spellbinding stars.

1³/₄lb/800g pumpkin, peeled and diced	¹/₄ teaspoon cayenne pepper
1 onion, chopped	1 pint/600ml water
1 tablespoon sunflower oil	¹/₂ pint/300ml fresh orange juice
¹/₂ teaspoon ground coriander	¹/₂ pint/300ml milk
¹/₂ teaspoon ground mace	roasted pumpkin seeds

Heat the oil and gently fry the onion until softened. Add the pumpkin, coriander, mace, cayenne pepper, water and orange juice and bring to the boil. Cover and simmer gently for 15 minutes until the pumpkin is tender. Allow to cool, then liquidise until smooth. Return to the cleaned out pan with the milk and reheat. Sprinkle some roasted pumpkin seeds in each bowlful when serving.

SPELLBINDING STARS (serves 8)

8 large slices medium cut sliced wholemeal bread	1 large garlic clove, crushed
1oz/25g vegetable margarine	¹/₂ teaspoon chives

Cut each slice of bread into four stars using a star-shaped biscuit cutter about 2¹/₂ inch/6cm across. Mix the margarine with the garlic and chives and spread carefully onto the stars. Put the stars on a baking tray and bake in a preheated oven at 180°C/350°F/Gas mark 4 for approximately 10 minutes until golden. Turn over once during the cooking time to brown both sides.

WITCHES' FINGERS (makes 8)

4oz/100g celery, finely chopped
2oz/50g ground almonds
2oz/50g mixed nuts, finely chopped
2oz/50g mushrooms, wiped and finely
  chopped
2oz/50g fresh wholemeal breadcrumbs
1oz/25g Cheddar cheese, grated
1oz/25g raisins
1/2oz/15g sesame seeds
1 small onion, finely chopped

1 egg, beaten
1 garlic clove, crushed
1 tablespoon sunflower oil
1 teaspoon soy sauce
1 teaspoon parsley
1 teaspoon thyme
1 teaspoon tahini
1/2 teaspoon paprika
black pepper
8 split almonds

Heat the oil and gently fry the onion, celery and garlic until softened. Remove from the heat, add the remaining ingredients except the split almonds and season with black pepper. Mix thoroughly until the mixture binds together. Divide into 8 equal piles on a large greased baking tray. Shape the piles into irregular knobbly finger shapes to represent witches' fingers. Push a split almond into one end of each 'finger' to resemble a finger nail. Bake in a preheated oven at 170°C/325°F/Gas mark 3 for about 35 minutes until golden. Serve either hot or cold.

VAMPIRE DIP (serves 8)

Choose a really dark red pepper to achieve a good red colour. This dip can be made the day before or on the morning of the party and refrigerated.

8oz/225g red pepper, chopped
3oz/75g redcurrant sauce
1 ripe tomato, skinned and chopped
1 small onion, finely chopped
2 garlic cloves, crushed

2 tablespoons water
1 tablespoon tomato purée
1 tablespoon sunflower oil
1/2 teaspoon paprika
black pepper

Heat the oil and gently fry the pepper, onion and garlic until soft. Add the tomato, water, tomato purée and paprika and season with black pepper. Simmer gently for a couple of minutes. Remove from the heat and allow to cool slightly. Add the redcurrant sauce and liquidise until smooth. Transfer to a serving bowl, cover and chill for a few hours before serving. Serve with witches' fingers.

STUFFED WIZARDS' HATS (makes 8)

These hats can be made in advance and frozen. Arrange the cooked frozen cones on a baking sheet, cover with foil and place in a preheated oven at 170°C/325°F/Gas mark 3 for about 30 minutes until heated through.

6oz/175g puff pastry	1 small onion, finely chopped
4oz/100g mushrooms, wiped and finely chopped	1 dessertspoon sunflower oil
	1 teaspoon parsley
2oz/50g smoked Cheddar cheese, grated	black pepper
1oz/25g hazelnuts, grated	

Heat the oil and gently fry the onion until softened. Add the mushrooms and fry until the juices run. Take off the heat and add the cheese, hazelnuts and parsley and season with black pepper.

Roll out the pastry into a 14 × 10 inch/35 × 25cm rectangle and cut into 8 strips measuring 14 × 1¼ inch/35 × 3cm. Grease 8 5 inch/13cm cone tins, then wind the pastry around loosely, beginning at the pointed end and overlapping slightly. Dampen the edge that overlaps with milk. Place on a greased baking tray and allow to rest for 15 minutes. Bake in a preheated oven at 170°C/325°F/Gas mark 3 for 15 minutes.

Take out of the oven and carefully remove the pastry cones from the tins. Fill each one with some of the filling, gently pressing it down to the point. Cover with foil and return to the oven for 25 minutes until the pastry is golden and the filling is heated through.

DEVILLED POTATO BUGS (makes 8)

8 potatoes, each weighing approx. 8oz/225g	2oz/50g Cheddar cheese, grated
	8 radishes, halved
4 tomatoes, sliced	16 raisins
16 slices of cucumber	8 cocktail sticks
1 punnet of mustard and cress, trimmed	vegetable margarine

Scrub the potatoes and cut 3 evenly spaced slits widthways across each one to within ½ inch/1cm of the base. Place the potatoes on a lightly greased baking tray and bake in a preheated oven at 220°C/425°F/Gas mark 7 for about 1 hour.

Cut each cocktail stick in half. Thread a raisin and half a radish onto each stick and press 2 sticks into one end of each potato to resemble eyes. Put a small amount of margarine into each slit in the potatoes and stuff the slits with the tomato and cucumber slices, mustard and cress and grated cheese. Serve immediately.

SPOOKY SWEET AND SOUR BEETROOT (serves 8)

1½lb/675g freshly cooked beetroot

sauce
3 fl.oz/75ml fresh orange juice
2 fl.oz/50ml light malt vinegar
1 tablespoon sweet sherry

1 tablespoon finely grated orange peel
1 dessertspoon soy sauce
1 rounded teaspoon arrowroot
1 teaspoon black mustard seeds
black pepper

Peel the beetroot and cut into thick strips. Place all the sauce ingredients in a saucepan and stir well until the arrowroot dissolves. Bring to the boil whilst stirring and continue stirring until the sauce thickens. Add the beetroot and mix until it is coated with sauce.

This dish can be served either hot or cold. To serve hot simply continue cooking on a low heat whilst stirring until the beetroot has heated through. To serve cold add the beetroot to the sauce and then refrigerate.

GHOULS' EYES (makes 32)

32 dessert dates, stoned
2oz/50g sunflower seeds, ground
2oz/50g quark
1 dessertspoon tahini

1 dessertspoon soy sauce
black pepper
32 raisins

Slit the dates lengthwise on one side and open them out slightly. Mix the ground sunflower seeds with the quark, tahini and soy sauce and season with black pepper. Stuff the dates with this mixture and top each stuffed date with a raisin, to look like an 'eye'.

MAGIC STONES SALAD (serves 8)

8oz/225g cooked chick peas
8oz/225g frozen peas
8oz/225g sweetcorn kernels
4oz/100g raisins
fresh chives, chopped

dressing
3 tablespoons light malt vinegar
1 tablespoon olive oil
1 dessertspoon soy sauce
black pepper

Cook the frozen peas and sweetcorn, then rinse under a cold tap. Drain and put in a bowl with the chick peas and raisins. Mix the dressing ingredients and pour over the salad. Toss, transfer to a serving bowl and garnish with fresh chopped chives. Refrigerate for a couple of hours before serving.

DEMON COCKTAIL BITES (makes approx. 60)

These little cocktail bites can be made the day before and stored in an airtight container.

4oz/100g fine wholemeal self raising
  flour
1oz/25g walnuts, grated
1oz/25g Cheddar cheese, grated
1oz/25g quark
1 fl.oz/25ml olive oil
2 tablespoons milk
1 rounded tablespoon grated Parmesan
  cheese

1 tablespoon onion seeds
1 teaspoon mixed herbs
1/2 teaspoon mustard powder
black pepper
milk
sesame seeds and poppy seeds

Mix the flour with the walnuts, Cheddar, Parmesan, onion seeds, mixed herbs, mustard powder and black pepper. Add the olive oil, quark and milk and mix until a soft dough is formed. Knead well and roll out on a floured board to 1/4 inch/5mm thick. Cut into various shapes using tiny cocktail cutters. Re-roll the dough as necessary until it is all used up. Place the shapes on a greased baking sheet, brush the tops with milk and sprinkle with sesame and poppy seeds. Bake in a preheated oven at 180°C/350°F/Gas mark 4 for 12-15 minutes until golden. Allow to cool on a wire rack.

BLACK SUNDAES (makes 8)

Make the sundaes on the morning of the party and add the yoghurt and grapes just before serving.

6 fl.oz/175ml blackcurrant juice drink
14 fl.oz/400ml water
2 teaspoons agar agar
4oz/100g frozen blackcurrants, thawed
2 fl.oz/50ml water
1 tablespoon demerara sugar

1 pint/600ml milk
2 rounded tablespoons custard powder
2 5oz/150g cartons of black cherry
  yoghurt
4 black grapes, halved

Mix the blackcurrant juice drink with the 14 fl.oz/400ml water and add the agar agar. Stir until this dissolves and no lumps remain. Transfer to a saucepan and heat until just below boiling point, stirring continuously. Divide between 8 serving glasses. Cover and refrigerate for a couple of hours until set.

Put the blackcurrants, 2 fl.oz/50ml water and the sugar in a small saucepan. Cook gently until pulpy. Dissolve the custard powder in the milk, add the blackcurrant pulp and liquidise until smooth. Transfer to a saucepan, bring to the boil whilst stirring and continue stirring until the custard thickens. Pour over the jelly in the glasses. Cover and refrigerate for a few hours until set. Spread the yoghurt over the top and garnish each sundae with half a black grape to serve.

A GUY FAWKES SUPPER

◊   ◊   ◊

After standing out in the cold watching the fireworks your guests will really appreciate a hot welcoming meal to come back to, served perhaps, with a warming glass of mulled red wine cup (see p.114).

A GUY FAWKES SUPPER MENU FOR 8

Chestnut and mushroom paté served with warm crusty French bread

Savoury pinwheels
Jacket potatoes with spicy baked bean filling
Mixed vegetable salad

Apple and banana charlotte served with yoghurt or ice cream

CHESTNUT AND MUSHROOM PATÉ (serves 8)

12oz/350g shelled chestnuts	2 tablespoons sherry
12oz/350g mushrooms, wiped and finely chopped	1 rounded teaspoon chervil
	1 teaspoon green pepper berries, crushed
3oz/75g fresh wholemeal breadcrumbs	1 dessertspoon Worcester sauce
1 onion, finely chopped	$^1/_2$ teaspoon yeast extract
1 tablespoon sunflower oil	black pepper
2 eggs	1 mushroom, sliced, to garnish

Steam the chestnuts until tender, then mash. Heat the oil and gently fry the onion until softened. Add the mushrooms and fry for 1 minute whilst stirring, then remove from the heat. Beat the eggs with the yeast extract and add to the pan together with the mashed chestnuts and remaining ingredients, except the sliced mushroom. Mix thoroughly and spoon into an 8 inch/20cm ovenproof dish. Press down firmly and level the top. Cover with foil and bake in a preheated oven at 180°C/350°F/Gas mark 4 for 1 hour. Remove the foil and bake for a further 30 minutes until browned on top. Serve in the dish and garnish with the sliced mushroom. Spread onto warm crusty French bread.

SAVOURY PINWHEELS (serves 8)

pastry
1lb/450g plain wholemeal flour
1 sachet easy-blend yeast
2oz/50g sunflower margarine, melted
1 egg, beaten
7 fl.oz/200ml milk, warmed
1 rounded tablespoon grated Parmesan
  cheese

filling
8oz/225g tomatoes, skinned and
  chopped
4oz/100g courgette, grated

4oz/100g mushrooms, wiped and
  chopped
2oz/50g red pepper, finely chopped
2oz/50g frozen chopped cooked spinach,
  thawed
2oz/50g Cheddar cheese, grated
1 onion, finely chopped
2 garlic cloves, crushed
1 tablespoon olive oil
1 rounded teaspoon oregano
1 rounded teaspoon thyme
1 rounded teaspoon parsley
black pepper

Mix the Parmesan cheese and yeast with the flour. Add the melted margarine, egg and milk and mix until a soft dough is formed. Knead well, place in a bowl and cover. Leave in a warm place for 1 hour.

Heat the oil for the filling and gently fry the onion and garlic until softened, then remove from the heat. Put the spinach in a sieve and squeeze out any excess water. Add to the onion and garlic together with the remaining filling ingredients and season with black pepper.

Turn the pastry out onto a floured board and knead well. Roll out to an oblong shape measuring 17 × 11 inch/43 × 28cm. Spread the filling evenly over the pastry, leaving a 1 inch/2¹/₂cm strip along one of the long edges for joining. Roll the pastry up like a Swiss roll to enclose the filling starting at the other long edge. Dampen the edge with milk and press together to join. Cut through with a sharp knife into 16 equal slices. Put the slices flat on a greased baking tray. Bake in a preheated oven at 180°C/350°F/Gas mark 4 for 30 minutes until golden.

JACKET POTATOES WITH SPICY
BAKED BEANS (serves 8)

8 potatoes, each weighing approx. 8oz/
  225g

filling
2 15¹/₂oz/440g tins baked beans in
  tomato sauce
1 onion, finely chopped
2 garlic cloves, crushed
1 dessertspoon vegetable oil

2 tablespoons raisins
1 dessertspoon Worcester sauce
1 dessertspoon soy sauce
¹/₄ teaspoon cayenne pepper
¹/₄ teaspoon paprika
black pepper

Scrub the potatoes and cut a large cross in the top of each one. Place the potatoes on a greased baking tray and bake in a preheated oven at 220°C/425°F/Gas mark 7 for about 1 hour until cooked.

Heat the oil and gently fry the onion and garlic until soft. Add the remaining filling ingredients, season with black pepper and cook gently until heated. Cut through the crosses on the potatoes and fill each one with the spicy baked bean filling.

MIXED VEGETABLE SALAD (serves 8)

4oz/100g cauliflower, cut into tiny florets
4oz/100g frozen sweetcorn kernels
4oz/100g frozen broad beans
4oz/100g frozen stringless cut green
  beans
3oz/75g carrot, scraped
2oz/50g mushrooms, wiped and sliced
2oz/50g leek, sliced
2oz/50g turnip, peeled
1oz/25g red pepper

1oz/25g yellow pepper
1oz/25g green pepper
1 stick of celery
2 gherkins, sliced
3 tablespoons white wine vinegar
1 dessertspoon sunflower oil
1 tablespoon fresh chives, chopped
few sprigs of fresh parsley, chopped
black pepper
Chinese leaves, shredded

Steam the cauliflower, sweetcorn, broad beans and green beans for 5 minutes, then rinse under cold running water. Drain and put in a mixing bowl. Cut the carrot, turnip, red, yellow and green peppers and celery into strips and add to the bowl together with the mushrooms, leek and gherkins. Season well with black pepper and add the chopped chives and parsley.

Mix the vinegar with the oil and pour over the salad. Toss well. Arrange the shredded Chinese leaves in a serving bowl and spread the salad on top. Cover and chill before serving.

APPLE AND BANANA CHARLOTTE (serves 8)

8oz/225g fresh wholemeal breadcrumbs
2oz/50g vegetable margarine
1oz/25g demerara sugar
1 rounded teaspoon ground cinnamon
2lb/900g cooking apples, peeled, cored
    and chopped

2oz/50g sultanas
1 tablespoon lemon juice
1 tablespoon maple syrup
2 large bananas, peeled and chopped

Melt the margarine in a large saucepan. Stir in the breadcrumbs, cinnamon and sugar and cook for a few minutes whilst stirring. Set aside.

Put the apple, sultanas, lemon juice and maple syrup in another saucepan and cook gently until the apple begins to soften. Remove from the heat and stir in the chopped banana.

Spread half the fruit mixture into a 12 × 6 inch/30 × 15cm casserole dish. Top with half the crumb mixture and spread it out evenly. Repeat these layers, then cover with foil. Bake in a preheated oven at 180°C/350°F/Gas mark 4 for 15 minutes. Remove the foil and bake for a further 15 minutes until golden. Serve with yoghurt or ice cream.

CELEBRATION DRINKS

◊   ◊   ◊

Home-made drinks are very easy to prepare and when served at your celebration can help make it that little bit more special. Long cool refreshing drinks are suitable for summer celebrations, while punches and mulled drinks are ideal for the winter.

Make your drinks look as good as they taste, with imaginative garnishing. Slices of fresh fruit, such as oranges, lemons, lime, star fruit and pineapple, always look appetising, either floating on top of the drink or placed on the edge of the glass. Pieces of fruit threaded onto cocktail sticks and resting on the rim of the glass also look attractive. Freshly picked mint leaves and nasturtium flowers make suitable garnishes for summer drinks. Brightly coloured paper umbrellas and bendy straws can be added to drinks for children.

This section contains a selection of alcoholic and non-alcoholic drinks, so that all your guests' tastes can be catered for.

TROPICAL BANANA LASSI (serves 6)

2 ripe bananas, peeled and chopped	1 pint/600ml tropical fruit juice
2 5oz/150g cartons of natural yoghurt	ground cinnamon

Liquidise the bananas with the yoghurt and fruit juice until smooth. Pour into 6 tumblers and sprinkle lightly with ground cinnamon to serve.

FRUITY CIDER PUNCH (serves 18)

2 pints/1.15 litres medium sweet cider	1 small orange
1 pint/600ml fresh orange juice	10 cloves
1 pint/600ml freshly brewed tea	1 apple, cored and sliced
½ pint/300ml brandy	1 kiwi fruit, peeled and sliced
4 inch/10cm cinnamon stick, broken in half	orange or lemon slices

Allow the tea to cool, then mix it with the cider, orange juice and brandy in a punch bowl. Scrub the orange well and stud with the cloves. Add to the punch bowl together with the cinnamon stick, apple and kiwi slices. Cover and refrigerate for a couple of hours until cold. Ladle the punch into glasses and garnish each glass with a slice of orange or lemon.

CRANBERRY AND APPLE SPRITZER (serves 6)

¹/₂ pint/300ml fresh cranberry juice
¹/₂ pint/300ml fresh apple juice

¹/₂ pint/300ml sparkling white wine
1 red eating apple, cored and sliced

Mix the cranberry juice with the apple juice and wine and chill until cold.
Pour into wine goblets and garnish each one with a slice of apple.

APRICOT AND ORANGE NECTAR (serves 4)

2oz/50g dried apricots
³/₄ pint/450ml fresh orange juice

¹/₂ pint/300ml white wine
4 slices of orange

Place the apricots and orange juice in a saucepan and bring to the boil.
Cover and simmer for 5 minutes. Allow to cool, then add the wine and
liquidise until smooth. Refrigerate until cold. Pour into 4 tumblers and
decorate each glass with a slice of orange. Add crushed ice if desired.

PINEAPPLE AND COCONUT CRUSH (serves 4)

1 8oz/225g tin of pineapple chunks in
    natural juice
2oz/50g desiccated coconut
³/₄ pint/450ml boiling water

¹/₂ pint/300ml fresh pineapple juice
4 glacé cherries, washed and dried
crushed ice

Pour the boiling water over the coconut. Cover and allow to stand for 2
hours. Strain the coconut water into a liquidiser, pressing out all the liquid,
and discard the coconut. Reserve 4 pineapple chunks for garnish, place the
remaining chunks together with the juice from the tin and the fresh
pineapple juice into the liquidiser and blend with the coconut water until
smooth. Strain into a large jug and refrigerate until cold. Whisk, then pour
into 4 tumblers. Thread a pineapple chunk and a glacé cherry onto a
cocktail stick and rest one stick on each glass. Add some crushed ice and
serve.

MULLED RED WINE CUP (serves 6)

1 bottle of red wine
2 fl.oz/50ml medium sherry
1 dessertspoon clear honey
1 cinnamon stick

¹/₂ teaspoon allspice berries
¹/₂ teaspoon cloves
1 lemon, sliced

Place all the ingredients apart from the lemon into a saucepan and heat
gently to just below boiling point. Strain into glasses and top each glass with
a lemon slice to serve.

RASPBERRY AND ORANGE SMOOTHIE (serves 6)

8oz/225g raspberries
1¹/₂ pint/900ml fresh orange juice
2¹/₂oz/65g raspberry flavoured fromage
  frais

6 slices of orange

Liquidise the raspberries with the orange juice. Pass through a sieve to remove the pips. Return the juice to the liquidiser, add the fromage frais and liquidise until smooth. Refrigerate for a couple of hours until cold, then whisk and pour into 6 tumblers. Garnish each glass with a slice of orange to serve.

MELON AND GINGER COCKTAIL (serves 6)

12oz/350g ripe melon, peeled and diced
1oz/25g stem ginger, chopped
³/₄ pint/450ml white wine

¹/₄ pint/150ml fresh apple juice
6 thin slices stem ginger
6 melon balls

Place the diced melon, chopped ginger, white wine and apple juice in a liquidiser and blend until smooth. Refrigerate until cold, then pour into 6 wine glasses. Thread a melon ball and a slice of stem ginger onto each of 6 cocktail sticks and rest these on the rim of each glass to serve.

PEACH PARADISE (serves 8)

4oz/100g dried peaches
1oz/25g sultanas
1 pint/600ml white grape juice

1³/₄ pint/1 litre carbonated mineral water
black and green grapes

Put the peaches and sultanas in a saucepan and cover with water. Allow to stand for 1 hour, then drain and rinse well. Return to the saucepan with the grape juice, bring to the boil, cover and simmer for 15 minutes. Allow to cool and liquidise until smooth, then refrigerate until cold. When cold add the carbonated mineral water and whisk until smooth. Pour into 8 tall glasses. Thread a couple of grapes onto cocktail sticks and rest on the rim of each glass to serve.

WHISKY AND MANDARIN TODDY (serves 6)

1 10oz/300g tin mandarins in natural
   juice
¹/₂ pint/300ml Norfolk Punch

¹/₄ pint/150ml fresh orange juice
¹/₄ pint/150ml whisky
orange slices

Put the mandarins and their juice in a liquidiser together with the Norfolk
Punch, orange juice and whisky. Liquidise until smooth, then transfer to a
saucepan. Heat until just warm and pour into 6 wine glasses. Garnish each
glass with a slice of orange.

KIWI AND APPLE FIZZ (serves 4)

1 large ripe kiwi fruit, peeled and
   chopped
8 fl.oz/225ml fresh apple juice

³/₄ pint/450ml sparkling apple juice,
   chilled
apple slices

Put the kiwi fruit and the fresh apple juice in a liquidiser and blend until
smooth. Strain into a large jug and refrigerate until cold. Add the chilled
sparkling apple juice and stir well. Pour into 4 tumblers and garnish each
with a slice of apple.

APRICOT AND ALMOND SHAKE (serves 6)

2oz/50g dried apricots
¹/₂ pint/300ml still mineral water
1 5oz/150g carton apricot flavoured
   yoghurt
1oz/25g ground almonds

1 teaspoon almond essence
1 pint/600ml carbonated mineral water,
   chilled
roasted flaked almonds

Wash the apricots thoroughly and put them in a small saucepan with the
still mineral water. Bring to the boil, cover and simmer until tender. Allow to
cool, then refrigerate until cold. Pour into a liquidiser with the yoghurt,
ground almonds, almond essence and carbonated mineral water and blend
until smooth. Pour into 6 tumblers and sprinkle a few roasted flaked
almonds on top of each drink.

HONEY, LEMON AND KIWI COOLER (serves 8)

1 lemon
1 pint / 600ml still mineral water
1 rounded tablespoon clear honey

2 large ripe kiwi fruits
1¹/₂ pints / 900ml carbonated mineral
   water, chilled

Scrub the lemon, cut in half and squeeze out the juice. Cut each lemon half into quarters and put in a saucepan together with the juice. Add the honey and still mineral water, stir well and bring to the boil. Cover and simmer for 5 minutes. Allow to cool, then strain into a liquidiser. Squeeze as much juice as possible from the lemon peel, then discard it. Peel and chop one of the kiwi fruits and add to the liquidiser. Blend until smooth and strain into a jug. Cover and refrigerate until cold.

Half fill 8 tumblers with the juice and top up with the chilled carbonated mineral water. Cut the other kiwi fruit into 8 slices and decorate each glass with a slice. Serve immediately.

HAZELNUT MOCHA FLIP (serves 4)

1oz / 25g hazelnuts, lightly roasted
1¹/₄ pints / 750ml milk
1 rounded tablespoon vanilla flavoured
   ice cream
1 rounded tablespoon carob powder,
   sieved

1 rounded dessertspoon decaffeinated
   coffee powder
1 teaspoon vanilla essence
grated carob

Place all the ingredients except the grated carob into a liquidiser and blend until smooth. Pass through a sieve into a large jug. Pour into 4 tumblers and sprinkle the top of each drink with grated carob.

ORANGE CIDER QUENCHER (serves 6)

1 pint / 600ml medium sweet cider
1 pint / 600ml fresh orange juice

crushed ice
orange slices

Mix the cider with the orange juice and pour into 6 tumblers. Add some crushed ice and a slice of orange to each glass.

PART 3
THE GIFT OF FOOD

A gift of home-made food makes a tasty and attractive present for a special friend or relation. The packaging for the gifts needn't be expensive, for with a little imagination and creativity gifts of food can be professionally presented.

Save empty glass jars, small boxes and baskets, cream cheese and ice cream containers, scraps of pretty cotton material, ribbons, doylies, coloured foil, wrapping and tissue paper, which can all be used to create pretty packaging for gifts.

Jars of preserves can be covered with mop caps cut from material or paper tied on with ribbon. Use a decorative label. Boxes and other cartons can be covered with wrapping paper or foil and lined with tissue paper and doylies. Decorate with ribbons, bows and rosettes.

For a really special gift make up a hamper of various home-made foods and package in a gaily decorated box or basket. Your gift can be personalised by adding a label saying 'Specially prepared for' and adding the recipient's name underneath.

Thin card can be used to make containers for small gifts to hang on the Christmas tree. Staple semi-circles of thin card into cone shapes, cover with wrapping paper and line with paper doylies. Attach a length of ribbon.

Remember that gifts of food make well-received presents at any time of the year and need not be confined to the festive season. Try to co-ordinate the packaging and labelling to suit the particular occasion you are celebrating.

MINIATURE CHRISTMAS CAKES (makes 12)

Miniature cake boards can be easily made by cutting out 12 3³/₄ inch/9¹/₂ cm circles from stiff card and covering them neatly with kitchen foil. Put a cake on each board and cover with clear cellophane.

6oz/175g fine wholemeal self raising flour
3oz/75g sunflower margarine
2oz/50g demerara sugar
2 eggs, beaten
10oz/300g mixed fruit
4oz/100g dried apricots, finely chopped
4oz/100g dried dates, finely chopped
4oz/100g glacé cherries, washed, dried and quartered
2oz/50g mixed cut peel
2oz/50g stem ginger, finely chopped
2oz/50g mixed nuts, chopped

2oz/50g ground almonds
1 rounded tablespoon malt extract
2 tablespoons brandy
1 teaspoon ground allspice
1 teaspoon ground mixed spice

to finish
approx. 6 teaspoons brandy
apricot jam
1¹/₂lb/675g marzipan

to decorate
12 plastic holly sprigs
red ribbon

Put all the fruit in a bowl and add the brandy. Stir well and allow to stand for 30 minutes. Cream the margarine with the sugar and malt extract. Add the beaten eggs and ground almonds and beat until smooth. Add the sifted flour and spices to the bowl of soaked fruit and stir well until the fruit is coated. Add the floured fruit and the mixed nuts to the other bowl and mix thoroughly. Divide the mixture between 12 deep, greased 3 inch/8cm ramekin dishes. Press down evenly and firmly. Cover with foil and bake for 1¹/₂ hours in a preheated oven at 150°C/300°F/Gas mark 2. Remove the foil and bake for a further 10-15 minutes until golden and firm in the centres. Turn out onto a wire rack and allow to cool.

When cool spoon about ¹/₂ teaspoonful of brandy over the top of each cake. Wrap them individually in foil and store in a cool place to mature for 2-3 weeks.

Spread the tops and sides of the cakes lightly with apricot jam. Divide the marzipan into 12 equal pieces and roll each piece out into a circle big enough to cover the top and sides of a cake. Tie a piece of red ribbon around and place a holly sprig on top of each cake.

MINIATURE SIMNEL CAKES

Make exactly like the Christmas cakes and add 11 tiny marzipan balls around the top of the marzipaned cakes. Place the cakes under a hot grill for a minute or two until the marzipan begins to brown slightly. Tie a yellow ribbon around each cake and decorate with a fluffy chick cake decoration.

WALNUT FLORENTINES (makes 20)

Present the florentines neatly packaged in a box lined with foil and covered with cellophane.

2oz/50g fine wholemeal self raising flour
2oz/50g sunflower margarine
2oz/50g glacé cherries, finely chopped
2oz/50g cut mixed peel, finely chopped
1oz/25g walnuts, grated

$^1/_2$oz/15g demerara sugar
1 tablespoon honey
1 tablespoon milk
$^1/_4$ teaspoon ground cinnamon
sesame seeds

Put the margarine, honey and sugar in a saucepan and heat until melted. Remove from the heat and add the remaining ingredients. Mix well. Place rounded teaspoonfuls of the mixture onto a greased baking tray. Press down to flatten and sprinkle with sesame seeds. Bake in a preheated oven at 180°C/350°F/Gas mark 4 for 10-12 minutes until golden. Cool on a wire rack, taking great care in transferring the biscuits as they are very delicate.

ALMOND FLORENTINES

Omit the walnuts and cinnamon from the ingredients for walnut florentines and replace them with 1oz/25g chopped flaked almonds and a few drops of almond essence.

FRUIT AND NUT TRUFFLES (makes approx. 25)

Little baskets lined with gold or silver doylies make ideal containers for truffles, petit fours and chews. Cover tightly with cling film or cellophane and decorate each basket with ribbon or a rosette.

2oz/50g dried apricots	1oz/25g ground almonds
2oz/50g dried dates	1oz/25g walnuts, grated
2oz/50g sultanas	1oz/25g sunflower margarine
2oz/50g raisins	2 tablespoons sherry
2oz/50g carob bar, broken	2 tablespoons dark rum
2oz/50g bran flakes, crushed	roasted flaked almonds, finely chopped

Chop all the fruit finely and place in a lidded container. Add the sherry and stir well. Put the lid on and leave for a few hours.

Place the broken carob bar and margarine in a large saucepan, heat until melted, then stir in the rum. Add the soaked fruit, ground almonds, walnuts and crushed bran flakes and mix thoroughly.

Take heaped teaspoonfuls of the mixture and form into balls. Roll each ball in the chopped flaked almonds until completed covered. Place the truffles on a plate, cover and refrigerate until set. Transfer to petit four cases.

CAROB TRUFFLES (makes approx. 16)

2oz/50g fine wholemeal self raising flour	2oz/50g carob bar, broken
1oz/25g demerara sugar	1oz/25g sunflower margarine
1 egg	2 tablespoons brandy
2 tablespoons milk	carob powder, desiccated coconut or
1 tablespoon carob powder	chocolate vermicelli
1 rounded teaspoon baking powder	

Whisk the egg with the sugar until light and frothy. Fold in the sifted flour, baking powder and carob powder. Stir in the milk and pour into a greased 8 inch/20cm sandwich tin. Bake in a preheated oven at 180°C/350°F/Gas mark 4 for about 15 minutes until springy. Turn out onto a wire rack and allow to cool.

Crumble the sponge into crumbs. Place the broken carob bar and margarine into a saucepan, heat gently until melted and stir in the brandy. Add the cake crumbs and mix thoroughly. Take heaped teaspoonfuls of the mixture and shape into small balls. Roll in carob powder, desiccated coconut or chocolate vermicelli. Place the truffles on a plate and cover. Refrigerate until set, then transfer to petit four cases.

CRISPY CHOCOLATE PETIT FOURS (makes 28)

3oz/75g milk chocolate bar
2oz/50g bran flakes, crushed
1oz/25g desiccated coconut
1oz/25g ground almonds

1oz/25g glacé cherries, finely chopped
1oz/25g raisins
1 rounded dessertspoon hazelnut and
   chocolate spread

Break the chocolate bar into small pieces and put in a saucepan with the hazelnut and chocolate spread. Heat gently whilst stirring until the chocolate melts. Add the remaining ingredients and mix thoroughly. Divide the mixture between 28 petit four cases. Press down evenly, cover and refrigerate for a few hours until set.

ALMOND PETIT FOURS (makes 20)

2oz/50g ground almonds
2oz/50g fine wholemeal self raising flour
1¹/₂oz/40g sunflower margarine, melted
1oz/25g demerara sugar

1 egg
1 tablespoon milk
1 teaspoon almond essence
20 split almonds

Put the egg, sugar and almond essence in a mixing bowl and whisk until light and frothy. Stir in the melted margarine and milk and fold in the ground almonds and flour. Divide the mixture between 20 petit four cases and place a split almond on top. Bake in a preheated oven at 180°C/350°F/Gas mark 4 for about 15 minutes until golden. Cool on a wire rack.

MUESLI AND HONEY CHEWS (makes 18)

4oz/100g fruit and nut muesli
2oz/50g carob bar, broken

1 rounded tablespoon honey
¹/₂oz/15g sunflower margarine

Put the carob bar, honey and margarine in a saucepan and heat gently until melted. Stir in the muesli and mix until well coated. Divide the mixture between 18 petit four cases and press down lightly. Cover and refrigerate for a few hours until set.

FRUITY LIQUEUR AND COCONUT CHEWS (makes approx. 30)

2oz/50g sultanas
2oz/50g raisins
2oz/50g currants
2oz/50g dried dates

2oz/50g desiccated coconut
2oz/50g ground almonds
2 tablespoons fruit flavoured liqueur
1oz/25g desiccated coconut, roasted

Mince all the fruit and put it in a mixing bowl. Work in the 2oz/50g desiccated coconut and the ground almonds. Add the liqueur and stir until the mixture binds together. Take rounded teaspoonfuls of the mixture and roll into small balls or sausage shapes. Roll each shape in the roasted coconut until covered. Place in petit four cases.

MINI COCONUT MACAROONS (makes 20)

Mini coconut macaroons and Almond kisses can be presented in wide-mouthed airtight jars. Add mop caps tied on with ribbon and a label.

2 egg whites
2oz/50g ground almonds
2oz/50g desiccated coconut

1oz/25g golden icing sugar
almond flakes
rice paper

Whisk the egg whites until stiff. Fold in the ground almonds, desiccated coconut and sifted icing sugar. Line a baking tray with rice paper. Spoon 20 heaps of the mixture onto the lined tray and flatten each one with a fork. Place a flaked almond on top of each macaroon and bake in a preheated oven at 180°C/350°F/Gas mark 4 for 15-20 minutes until golden. Tear the rice paper round the edges of the macaroons and allow them to cool on a wire rack.

ALMOND KISSES (makes approx. 30)

2oz/50g ground almonds
2oz/50g vegetable margarine
1oz/25g cornflour
1oz/25g ground brown rice

1oz/25g golden icing sugar
1 teaspoon almond essence
flaked almonds

Cream the margarine with the icing sugar and almond essence. Work in the cornflour, ground almonds and ground brown rice until smooth. Place the mixture in an icing bag which is fitted with a star-shaped nozzle. Pipe 30 stars onto a lightly greased baking sheet and press a flaked almond on top of each one. Bake in a preheated oven at 180°C/350°F/Gas mark 4 for 8-10 minutes until just golden. Allow to cool on a wire rack.

SAVOURY OATCAKES (makes approx. 24)

These little oatcakes can simply be wrapped in coloured cellophane tied with ribbon to present. Add a label saying that they are delicious served with cheese or a savoury topping.

4oz/100g medium oatmeal	2 fl.oz/50ml hot water
2oz/50g fine wholemeal self raising flour	1 dessertspoon tahini
¹/₂oz/15g vegetable margarine	¹/₂ teaspoon yeast extract

Melt the margarine over a low heat. Remove from the heat and add the oatmeal and flour. Dissolve the tahini and yeast extract in the hot water and add to the pan. Mix well until a soft dough is formed. Roll out on a lightly floured board to about ¹/₈ inch/3mm thick. Cut into 2 inch/5cm squares using a biscuit cutter. Gather up the remaining dough and repeat until it is all used. Place the squares on a greased baking sheet and bake in a preheated oven at 180°C/350°F/Gas mark 4 for approximately 10 minutes until golden. Allow to cool on a wire rack.

'CHRISTMAS PUDDING' TRUFFLES (makes 12)

These fruit truffles resemble Christmas puddings topped with 'cream' and edible 'holly'. Line a shallow box with Christmas paper as a container for these truffles. Cover with cling film or cellophane and decorate with tinsel and small Christmas stickers.

4oz/100g no-soak, ready-to-eat figs, washed and dried	1 rounded teaspoon ground mixed spice
	chocolate vermicelli
4oz/100g dessert dates, stoned	¹/₂oz/15g icing sugar
4oz/100g sultanas	¹/₂ teaspoon almond essence
4oz/100g raisins	1 teaspoon lemon juice
1oz/25g ground almonds	2 glacé cherries, washed and dried
1oz/25g walnuts, grated	2 inch/5cm length angelica
2 tablespoons brandy	

Mince the figs, dates, sultanas and raisins. Put in a mixing bowl with the ground almonds, walnuts, brandy and ground mixed spice and mix thoroughly. Divide the mixture into 12 equal pieces, form each one into a ball and roll in the chocolate vermicelli. Transfer the truffles to petit four cases.

Mix the icing sugar with the almond essence and lemon juice until smooth. Spoon a small amount of icing on top of each truffle. Cut the glacé cherries into 12 pieces. Place a piece of cherry on top of the icing with a couple of slivers of angelica, to resemble holly berries and leaves.

LEMON AND GINGER HEART COOKIES (makes approx. 25)

These little heart-shaped biscuits make an appropriate gift for Valentine's Day.

2oz/50g fine wholemeal self raising flour	2oz/50g vegetable margarine
2oz/50g porridge oats	1oz/25g stem ginger, very finely chopped
2oz/50g ground brown rice	2 rounded tablespoons lemon curd

Cream the margarine with the lemon curd and work in the remaining ingredients until a soft dough is formed. Wrap the dough in cling film and chill in the refrigerator for 30 minutes.

Turn it out onto a floured board and roll out thinly. Cut into heart shapes using a small heart-shaped biscuit cutter. Gather up the leftover dough and repeat until all the dough is used up. Place the hearts on a lightly greased baking sheet and bake in a preheated oven at 170°C/325°F/Gas mark 3 for about 15 minutes until just golden. Cool on a wire rack.

FRUITY CHOCOLATE LOG

A log mould can be made by cutting a $8^{1}/_{2} \times 7$ inch/22 $\times$ 18cm oblong from thin card and covering one side with kitchen foil. Join the long edges together with sellotape with the foil on the inside. Cover one end of the resulting 7 inch/18cm tube with a piece of cling film and stick it in place.

6oz/175g milk chocolate bar, broken	1oz/25g sultanas
2oz/50g bran flakes, crushed	1oz/25g raisins
2oz/50g desiccated coconut	1oz/25g sunflower margarine
2oz/50g plain sweet biscuits, broken into small pieces	3 tablespoons brandy or dark rum
2oz/50g dried dates, finely chopped	1 rounded tablespoon honey
2oz/50g dried apricots, finely chopped	1 teaspoon ground mixed spice
	cake decorations

Put 4oz/100g of the chocolate bar in a large saucepan with the margarine and honey. Heat until melted, then stir in the brandy or rum. Add the bran flakes, coconut, broken biscuits, dates, apricots, sultanas, raisins and mixed spice. Mix thoroughly, then press the mixture evenly into a 7 inch/18cm log mould. Refrigerate for a few hours until set.

Remove the log from the mould and place it on a plate. Melt the remaining chocolate in a bowl over a pan of boiling water and spread it all over the log, using a fork to give a log effect. Return to the refrigerator until the chocolate has set.

Decorate with cake decorations and put on a board made from a piece of cardboard covered with foil. Cover with clear cellophane.

MARINATED FRUIT COCKTAIL

4oz / 100g raisins
4oz / 100g sultanas
2oz / 50g glacé cherries, quartered
2oz / 50g dried dates, finely chopped
2oz / 50g cut mixed peel

2oz / 50g dried apricots, finely chopped
1oz / 25g stem ginger, finely chopped
3 fl.oz / 75ml medium sherry
2 fl.oz / 50ml brandy

Put all the fruit in a lidded container, pour the sherry and brandy over and stir well. Put the lid on the container and store in a cool place for 2 days to allow the fruit to absorb the alcohol, stirring every now and again.

Transfer to small sterilised jars with lids, add decorative tops and labels. This fruit cocktail will keep for about 6 weeks, so put the 'use by' date on the labels. Add a note on the label saying that this mixture can be added to fruit salads to give a festive flavour, or used as a garnish on cheesecakes or simply spooned over ice cream or yoghurt for a quick dessert.

ORANGE AND DATE CHUTNEY (makes approx. 3lb / 1½kg)

1½lb / 675g oranges
8oz / 225g dried dates, finely chopped
½ pint / 300ml white wine vinegar
4oz / 100g onion, finely chopped
4oz / 100g demerara sugar

½ teaspoon ground coriander
½ teaspoon ground mace
¼ teaspoon ground cinnamon
¼ teaspoon cayenne pepper

Wash the oranges thoroughly, dry and chop very finely. Put in a large saucepan with the dates, onion and vinegar. Stir well, bring to the boil and simmer for 10 minutes. Take off the heat and add the rest of the ingredients. Bring back to the boil and simmer gently until the mixture thickens, stirring frequently to prevent sticking. Pour into warm sterilised jars, cover and label. This chutney will keep for about 3 months.

SPICED KUMQUATS (fills 3 8oz / 225g jars)

1lb / 450g kumquats, sliced
4oz / 100g demerara sugar
8 fl.oz / 225ml light malt vinegar
1 inch / 2¹/₂cm stick of cinnamon, broken

12 cloves
1 teaspoon allspice berries
2 cardamoms, husked and the seeds
  separated

Put the vinegar in a saucepan with the cinnamon, cloves, allspice berries and cardamoms. Bring to the boil, cover and simmer for 5 minutes. Strain the vinegar and discard the spices. Return the vinegar to the saucepan and stir in the sugar and kumquats. Bring to the boil and simmer gently until the kumquats are tender, stirring frequently to prevent sticking. Pour into clean warmed jars, cover and label. Spiced kumquats will keep for about 3 months.

PINEAPPLE AND GINGER CHUTNEY

(makes approx. 2lb / 900g)

1¹/₄lb / 550g pineapple, peeled and finely
  chopped
8oz / 225g onions, finely chopped
6oz / 175g cooking apple, peeled and
  grated
3oz / 75g demerara sugar
2oz / 50g stem ginger, finely chopped

2oz / 50g sultanas
6 fl.oz / 175ml light malt vinegar
¹/₄ teaspoon ground allspice
¹/₄ teaspoon ground cloves
¹/₄ teaspoon ground cinnamon
¹/₄ teaspoon ground coriander

Put the vinegar, sugar and spices into a large saucepan and stir until the sugar dissolves. Add the rest of the ingredients and stir well. Bring to the boil, then simmer gently until the mixture thickens, stirring frequently to prevent sticking. Pour into warm sterilised jars, cover and label. Keeps for about 3 months.

SPICED ORANGE SLICES (fills 3 1lb / 450g jars)

2lb / 900g oranges
1 pint / 600ml pickling vinegar
4oz / 100g light muscovado sugar
2 inch / 5cm stick of cinnamon

1 teaspoon cloves
$^1/_2$ teaspoon coriander seeds
$^1/_4$ teaspoon ground mace

Put the vinegar, sugar and spices in a large saucepan and stir until the sugar dissolves. Wash the oranges thoroughly, cut into $^1/_4$ inch / 5mm thick slices and remove the pips. Add to the pan and bring to the boil, cover and simmer gently until the orange peel is tender. Pack the orange slices into warm sterilised jars. Strain the vinegar and pour over the oranges, covering them completely. Cover and label the jars. Spiced orange slices are best used within 4 weeks, so put a 'use by' date on the label.

BOUQUET GARNI (makes 10)

These bouquet garni look attractive when presented in a small airtight jar.

10 $5^1/_2$ inch / 14cm circles of muslin
cotton
10 bay leaves

5 teaspoons each of parsley, thyme, rosemary, marjoram, chives, chervil, sage

Put the circles of muslin on a flat surface. Crumble each bay leaf into pieces and place these in the centre of each circle, together with $^1/_2$ teaspoonful of each herb. Gather the muslin together to enclose the herbs and tie each one with cotton. Leave sufficient cotton hanging so that the bags can be tied to saucepan handles.

MARINATED OLIVES (fills 2 small jars)

Use these olives as a garnish or add to salads or savoury dishes. The flavoured oil can be strained and used after the olives have been used.

8oz / 225g green or black olives
2 teaspoons pickling spices
4 dried chillis

2 bay leaves
2 garlic cloves, sliced
olive oil

Wash the olives and drain well. Pack them into 2 small sterilised jars with 1 teaspoon of pickling spice, 2 dried chillis, 1 bay leaf and 1 sliced garlic clove to each jar. Cover with olive oil to the top of the jars. Seal tightly and shake the jars to distribute the spices. Store in a cool place for at least 3 weeks before using.

VALENTINE TRUFFLE HEART

This rich truffle heart is rather time consuming to make, but well worth the effort to give to a special person on St. Valentine's Day.

8oz/225g marzipan
2oz/50g glacé cherries, washed, dried
  and quartered
2oz/50g hazelnuts, grated and roasted
2oz/50g raisins
1oz/25g sunflower margarine
4oz/100g carob bar, broken
1 tablespoon sherry

sponge
2oz/50g fine wholemeal self raising flour
1oz/25g demerara sugar
1 tablespoon carob powder
1 rounded teaspoon baking powder
1 egg
2 tablespoons milk

icing
1oz/25g icing sugar
approx. 1¹/₂ teaspoons lemon juice

First make the sponge. Whisk the egg with the sugar until light and frothy. Fold in the sifted flour, baking powder and carob powder. Stir in the milk and pour into a greased 8 inch/20cm sandwich tin. Bake in a preheated oven at 180°C/350°F/Gas mark 4 for about 15 minutes until springy. Turn out onto a wire rack and allow to cool.

Soak the raisins in the sherry for 30 minutes. Line a heart-shaped sandwich tin measuring approximately 7¹/₂ inch/19cm at the widest part with foil. Roll out the marzipan and use it to line the tin, leaving a slight overhang. Crumble the sponge into fine crumbs in a mixing bowl. Add the roasted hazelnuts, glacé cherries and soaked raisins. Melt the margarine with 2oz/50g of the carob bar in a large saucepan, remove from the heat and add the crumb mixture. Mix thoroughly and pile into the lined heart. Press down firmly and evenly and fold the overhanging marzipan towards the centre. Carefully invert the heart mould onto a baking tray and remove the foil. Melt the remaining carob bar in a bowl over a pan of boiling water and brush the carob over the marzipan, covering it completely. Refrigerate for a few hours until the carob has set.

Mix the icing sugar with enough lemon juice to make a thick paste and transfer it to an icing bag fitted with a fine writing nozzle. Write the name of the recipient or a message on the heart with the icing. Return it to the refrigerator until the icing has set. Transfer the heart to a cake board and cover it with cellophane.

HERB VINEGAR (makes 1 pint / 600ml)

Bottles of herb oils and vinegars make attractive gifts especially for enthusiastic cooks. They can be used for flavouring salads, salad dressings, sauces and marinades.

1 pint/600ml white wine vinegar	2oz/50g fresh herbs, basil, thyme, rosemary, sage or tarragon or a combination

Bruise the leaves of the herbs to release the flavour, then place in a wide-mouthed jar with the vinegar. Cover with a vinegar-proof lid and leave to infuse for at least 3 weeks. Shake the jar occasionally. Strain into decorative bottles and add a fresh sprig of the chosen herb. Seal and label.

HERB OIL (makes 1 pint / 600ml)

Follow the instructions for herb vinegar, but substitute olive or sunflower oil for the vinegar.

WHISKY AND HONEY MUSTARD
(makes 14oz / 400g)

2oz/50g yellow mustard seeds	2 tablespoons honey
2oz/50g black mustard seeds	4 tablespoons whisky
6 fl.oz/175ml white wine vinegar	

Put the mustard seeds and vinegar in a lidded container. Allow to stand for 2 days. Add the whisky and honey and stir well. Leave for 1 week. After this time blend until almost smooth. The texture should be thick and slightly crunchy. Transfer to small sterilised jars, cover and label. For a different flavour white wine can be substituted for the whisky.

SPICED NUTS

8oz/225g mixed shelled nuts	1/2 teaspoon ground coriander
1 tablespoon sunflower oil	1/4 teaspoon turmeric
1 teaspoon curry powder	black pepper

Put the oil and the spices in a shallow casserole dish or baking tin and stir. Add the nuts, season with black pepper and stir well until all the nuts are coated in oil and spices. Bake in a preheated oven at 170°C/325°F/Gas mark 3 for about 20 minutes until golden, stirring occasionally to ensure even browning. Allow to cool, then store in an airtight jar.

SAVOURY ROASTED SEEDS

2oz/50g sunflower seeds
2oz/50g pumpkin seeds
2 teaspoons sunflower oil

1 teaspoon soy sauce
$\frac{1}{2}$ teaspoon paprika
black pepper

Pour the sunflower oil and soy sauce in a shallow casserole dish and place in a preheated oven at 180°C/350°F/Gas mark 4 for 2 minutes to warm. Remove from the oven, stir in the seeds and paprika and season with black pepper. Stir well until all the seeds are coated. Return to the oven for 15 minutes until the seeds are just beginning to brown, stirring a couple of times during the cooking time. Allow to cool, then store in an airtight jar.

TRAIL MIX (makes 1lb / 450g)

An easy recipe for a tasty mixture that children will enjoy making.

4oz/100g raisins
4oz/100g shelled peanuts
2oz/50g roasted flaked coconut

2oz/50g pumpkin seeds
2oz/50g sunflower seeds
2oz/50g dried banana chips

Mix all the ingredients together and store in airtight jars.

FRUIT AND NUT MUESLI (makes 2lb / 900g)

4oz/100g jumbo oats
4oz/100g wheat flakes
4oz/100g rye flakes
4oz/100g barley flakes
2oz/50g raisins
2oz/50g sultanas
2oz/50g dried dates, chopped

2oz/50g glacé fruits, chopped (i.e. pineapple, papaya)
4oz/100g mixed nuts, chopped
2oz/50g dried banana chips
1oz/25g shredded coconut
1oz/25g wheatgerm

Mix all the ingredients together and store in an airtight jar. Add a label saying 'serve with stewed fresh fruit and milk or yoghurt'.

MALTED MUESLI (makes approx. 1¼lb / 550g)

1lb/450g fruit and nut muesli
2 rounded tablespoons malt extract

2 tablespoons sunflower oil

Put the malt extract and sunflower oil in a large saucepan and heat gently until the malt becomes runny and combines with the oil. Remove from the heat and add the muesli. Stir thoroughly until well coated. Tip into a baking tin and bake in a preheated oven at 140°C/275°F/Gas mark 1 for approximately 8 minutes until golden, stirring once or twice to ensure even browning. Loosen in the tin while still hot, then allow to cool. Store in an airtight jar. Add a label saying ' Delicious served with fruit and yoghurt for breakfast or as a dessert'.

CRUNCHY GRANOLA (makes 1lb / 450g)

2oz/50g porridge oats
2oz/50g muesli base flakes (i.e. wheat, barley and rye flakes)
2oz/50g mixed nuts, chopped
1oz/25g sunflower seeds
1oz/25g sesame seeds
1oz/25g pumpkin seeds

1oz/25g desiccated coconut
½oz/15g wheatgerm
½oz/15g bran
4 tablespoons sunflower oil
1 tablespoon malt extract
1 tablespoon honey

Put the oil, malt and honey in a large saucepan and heat gently until the malt and honey go runny and combine with the oil. Remove from the heat and stir in the rest of the ingredients. Mix thoroughly, then spread the mixture on a greased baking tray. Bake in a preheated oven at 140°C/275°F/Gas mark 1 for about 20 minutes until golden, stirring a few times during the cooking time. Allow to cool, then separate any large pieces with your fingers. Store in an airtight jar. Add a label saying 'Delicious served with fruit and yoghurt for breakfast or as a dessert'.

TRUFFLE FILLED EASTER EGGS (makes 2 eggs)

To make these filled eggs into an extra special present a personalised note for the recipient could be placed inside the egg before it is joined.

8oz/225g carob bar
fruit and nut truffles or carob truffles (see p.121)

4 5 inch/13cm long flexible Easter egg moulds

Rub the inside of the egg moulds with a clean tea towel to polish. Break the carob bar into pieces and melt in a bowl over a pan of simmering water. Divide most of the melted carob between the egg moulds and quickly swirl it around to cover the moulds completely and evenly. Reserve a little for re-melting to join the eggs together. Turn the filled moulds face down on a baking tray and refrigerate until set.

Gently ease the eggs out of the moulds. Place some crumpled or shredded tissue paper or cellophane in 2 half eggs and place some truffles on top. Re-melt the reserved carob, allow to cool slightly and brush around the edges of the filled eggs. Place the other egg halves on top and fill any gaps in the joins with more melted carob. Refrigerate until set.

Tie a ribbon around the filled eggs, wrap in cellophane and pack in pretty boxes.